A s a new vision of value chains, the **[...]** iform business architecture that applies to **[...]** es. In this book, the structure of the Dynamic Value Chain is defined and illustrated through case studies from large, well-known companies and smaller, regional businesses. New concepts are presented for the first time:

- A dual cycle business model underlies all types of businesses
- A company has one to many value chains that deliver value offerings to customers
- Every company has an innovation value chain
- Macro Performance Indicators can be used to optimize the business with multi-departmental initiatives.

With the value chain basics established, the foundations of competitive strategy from past business literature are reviewed and combined into three competitive strategies.

- A three-step process is described how to select the best competitive strategy for the Dynamic Value Chains in the business.
- Macro Performance Indicators are presented for each competitive strategy
- Advice is provided on how to optimize the specific Dynamic Value Chain elements to achieve competitive advantage and enduring profitability.

This book is provided to entrepreneurs, business practitioners, academics, and students to increase awareness of business constructs, and in the hope that additional research will be conducted to expand the abilities of the management team to visualize and optimize their business.

Visualizing and Optimizing Your Business

Dynamic Value Chains

David N. Culbreth

Dynamic Value Chains
© Copyright 2017, David N. Culbreth
All rights reserved.

Edited: Mira Perrizo
Cover and interior design: Rebecca Finkel, F + P Graphic Design

Library of Congress Control Number: 2017942476
ISBN hard cover: 978-0-9990286-0-5
ISBN soft cover: 978-0-9990286-1-2
ISBN ebook: 978-0-9990286-2-9

First Edition
Printed in USA

Contents

CHAPTER 1

Introduction

EARLY IN MY BUSINESS CAREER, I was presented with a challenge by my immediate manager to "See the big picture" of the technology software firm where I worked. Taking this challenge to heart I began a quest to discover the big picture of the company. When I approached the CEO with the suggestion of conducting a special project to define the big picture of the company, he was interested and enthusiastically supported the idea. The exercise yielded the first of many enterprise models and fired my passion for mapping businesses to understand the critical pathways for value production.

Over the years that followed, I was fortunate to work in a variety of businesses and the "big picture" view evolved into the Dynamic Value Chain, which integrates value chain and supply chain concepts in line with leading business publications. During my career as a business executive, the model has been used to develop startup businesses and improve existing businesses, as well as communicate the big picture of the business to executives in a new and dynamic manner. In developing this book, I worked with several friends who are CEOs and executive managers so I could include practitioner case studies, along with classic stories from leading corporations to illustrate key points.

Another insight that evolved over this time was the concept of Macro Performance Indicators. Rather than tens or even hundreds of Key Performance Indicators used by line managers and department heads to run their specific portion of the business, Macro Performance Indicators are a small set of "big dials" often spanning multiple departments that have a major effect on the business performance.

My desire is to share the Dynamic Value Chain concept and the Macro Performance Indicators with business practitioners, academic leaders, and students to increase knowledge of value chains and sustainable competitive advantage.

The Dynamic Value Chain provides insights that can be used to design, build, and optimize businesses. Chapter 2 and 3 describe the Dynamic Value Chain and its primary elements to present the holistic view of the business operational model or "clockwork" described in *Built to Last*, the prequel to *Good to Great* by Jim Collins. For readers that would like to explore the detail level of the five elements of the Dynamic Value Chain, Chapter 4 presents the specific elements in detail. The application of the Dynamic Value Chain to various production strategies in Chapter 5 expands the perspective of how companies operate at the CEO's 30,000-foot view. As described in Chapter 6, companies have more than one value chain that delivers offerings to their customers, including the innovation value chain, present in all companies, that creates new goods and services, and optimizes the business through improvement initiatives.

Moving outside the company, external distribution channels and supply chains are explored in Chapter 7 with the Dynamic Value Chains of retailers, resellers, distributors, and supply chains. Case examples from the automobile and grocery industries highlight the historical improvements in these business models. We shift gears in Chapter 8 to review the customer-driven strategies of competitive advantage, starting with Customer Perceived Value, to address the target of any company's value. From a historical perspective, the *competitive strategy* concepts of Michael Porter and then Treacy and Wiersema's *value discipline* concepts are reviewed. This chapter concludes with the key principal proposed by Treacy and Wiersema that long-term performance requires a company to excel in one value discipline (Operational Excellence, Product Leadership or Customer Intimacy) and remain competent in the other two disciplines.

A three-step process for a business to self-analyze and then select a competitive strategy is provided in Chapter 9, followed by a chapter on business optimization. The Dynamic Value Chain is provided for each of the three value discipline strategies in Chapter 10, along with techniques for the optimization of each value chain. As plans are developed to optimize the Dynamic Value Chain, the management team can take advantage of Marco Performance Indicators. Chapter 11 describes these Macro Performance Indicators (MPIs) that, when measured and optimized, are the *big dials of corporate performance* for each competitive strategy. These MPIs provide a few cross-departmental metrics versus hundreds of departmental-specific Key Performance Indicators (KPIs), to better align the firm for major improvements in competitive advantage and sustainable profitability.

Finally, it is my desire in this book to introduce the concepts of Dynamic Value Chains and Macro Performance Indicators with supporting case studies to provide new techniques for business visualization and optimization. To this end, research and collaboration is encourage to validate and expand the theories presented herein.

CHAPTER 2

Visualizing the Business

AN INTRIGUING CHALLENGE for executive teams in business enterprises is to visualize, understand, and optimize the specific operations of the company that add value for the customer. As Jim Collins and Jerry Porras pointed out in their book, *Built to Last,*[1] the leaders of visionary companies persisting over long periods of time tend to be "clock builders," focusing on optimizing their organization. This concept of the business organization as a clockwork has fascinated me for years, because it would follow that if there was a way to visualize the clockwork clearly and succinctly, then business leaders would be able to make changes to improve their operations and, subsequently, the value and sustainability of their business.

Michael Porter provided an activity-based model of the business clockwork in his seminal work, *Competitive Advantage,*[2] where he introduced the *Value Chain* concept—a set of value activities that are linked to deliver value (at the business unit level). The value activities can be constructed and optimized to provide differentiation and competitive advantage. For the first time, the Value Chain concept provided a linkage between a company's high level strategy and the detailed implementation of that strategy to achieve a competitive advantage and thus increase business value over time.

In 1985, Porter's value chain was a step beyond the currently accepted McKinsey and Company's business system concept, which focused on analyzing and improving the individual functional silos of the business such as marketing, sales, research and development, human resources, finance, operations, and distribution channels. The McKinsey approach sought to broadly improve all the major functions to improve the business, but overlooked the integrated flow of activities across the business. To increase product value and gain an advantage over competitors, the value chain provided a new tool with a cross-functional perspective (interdependent system) for analysis and improvement of the value activities that lead to customer value and profitability. Simply stated, Porter introduced a value-based model that could be used to optimize the business.

So what did this value-based model look like? Porter defined the value activities in two categories—primary and support activities. Primary value activities are the steps that produce, sell, and maintain the product: inbound logistics, operations, outbound logistics, marketing and sales, and services. Support activities include procurement, technology development, human resource management, and firm infrastructure, which includes general management, planning, finance, legal, accounting, and quality assurance.

EXHIBIT 2-1. **Porter's Value Chain**

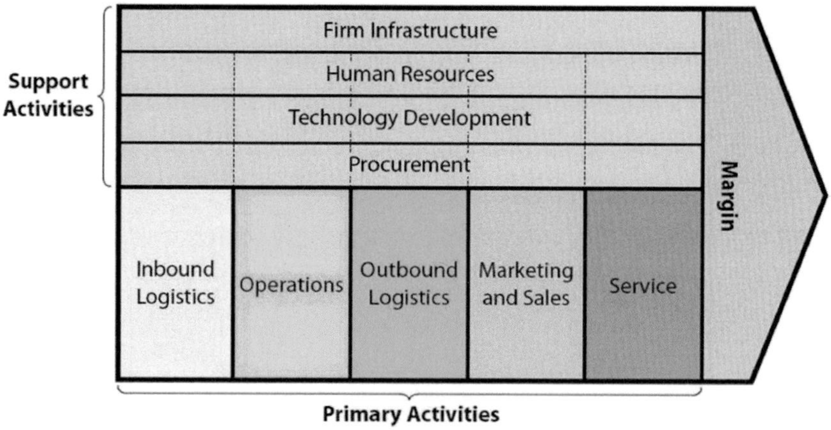

Applying this framework, a company's strategy would then shift from a high-level vision or mission statement to a distinct configuration of value activities aligned to deliver a specific mix of value to a chosen set of customers. Optimization of the value activities for strategic advantage is complex and time consuming, since the competencies of many related activities must be evaluated and improved with the overall strategy in mind. This requires strong top-down leadership and new ways of visualizing and understanding the entire business model in a cross-functional integrated way.

2.1 **Current Business Perspectives**

Today, executive teams rely on several widely-accepted tools to visualize, understand, and improve their business models. First, there is the *hierarchical organization chart* that presents the business as a team of functional departments with a chief executive leader at the top. Each departmental executive leader works to optimize their functional group based on group performance metrics, but these improvements tend to be siloed with less attention to the overall value chain perspective that runs through multiple departments. Conflicts emerge between departments that are pursuing their own objectives, which can detract from the business's ability to meet strategic goals.

Secondly, *financial and departmental reports* based on standardized accounting practices provide income statements, balance sheets, cash flow, and budget reports for the company, as well as specific departmental units. Profit and loss is a primary indicator of performance for the company and revenue generating business units. Supporting functions within the business, such as human resources and information technology departments, are treated as cost centers, where cost is continually being scrutinized and reduced, with the singular desire to lower cost rather than optimize the cross-departmental relationships and contributions to the value chain.

In addition, each department also has specific departmental reports that managers use to track and manage the performance of their team. In larger organizations, these measurements are codified into key performance indicators (KPIs) that are tracked over time as a trend line. As the usage of KPIs has evolved, a proliferation of these measurements in larger companies has occurred, which can overwhelm upper managers and make it difficult to see the truly impactful metrics—the big dials—that they can use to make effective changes across multiple departments.

Finally, there are the *operational procedures and diagrams* developed from process engineering that are applied to functional departments, such as R&D, manufacturing, and customer service, to capture the processes and seek process improvements. Business process reengineering (BPR) emerged as a management practice in the early 1990s to analyze and restructure a set of logically connected tasks performed to achieve a specific business outcome. Although BPR was envisioned as a corporate-wide view of the business process, many projects drilled down into the detailed operational processes to the point that they lost their high-level impact. In practice, due to the massive scale of the BPR changes, lack of executive commitment, extensive changes to supporting information systems, and extensive resistance to change within the workforce, it was found that by 1998 only 30 percent of BPR projects were deemed successful.[3]

The generally accepted business tools of organizational charts, financial and departmental reports, and operational procedures and diagrams provide the management team with tools to understand their business, but more is needed to drive optimization for lasting competitive strategy. For the business executive, visualizing the dynamic business model—a holistic, cross-functional model of the enterprise showing the value activities—is extremely useful in identifying areas for stronger integration and optimization.

The *Dynamic Value Chain* that is introduced in this book is a new, graphical view of the integrated value activities of the company—the value chain. Interestingly, as it is applied to different industries, the underlying structure of the Dynamic Value Chain remains constant, while the nomenclature of the value activities changes for each business type. The unified structure of the Dynamic Value Chain makes it easier for individual companies to map their specific business processes and terminology to a standard architectural view. Once a competitive strategy is defined, the Dynamic Value Chain and select Macro Performance Indicators become the tools that allow the management team to drive cross departmental changes leading to lasting competitive advantage and profitability.

CHAPTER 3

The Dynamic Value Chain Construct

AT THE CORPORATE LEVEL, the executive management team strives to see the entire business structure and make decisions that improve overall profits, customer loyalty, and competitive positioning. Due to the segmentation of the company into its functional departments, it is a challenge to clearly see the sequence of activities that add value to the company's goods and services, but doing so can bring new insights into the areas of strength and weakness along the value chain. The starting point for the Dynamic Value Chain perspective is to envision the activities that directly add value to the offerings, e.g. for a manufacturing company, as they are designed, developed, manufactured, sold, and installed. Activities that do not directly add value to the offerings are considered to be supporting activities in line with Porter's value chain concepts.

3.1 The Dynamic Value Chain

Corporate-level models that are used in describing the business have typically been either a horizontal roadmap of activities with a beginning and an end, or a circular arrangement of activities where the end joins back to the beginning of a single process cycle. As shown in Exhibit 3.1, the Dynamic Value Chain is comprised of several major elements including two major cycles—Order Fulfillment and Production. This dual cycle approach to envisioning the business is a key differentiation in the Dynamic Value Chain since the two major cycles run at different speeds to pull from inventory (Order Fulfillment) or place goods and services into inventory (Production).

At the top of the model is the target market with the customers who are candidates for the product or services that the company is selling. The Dynamic Value Chain is highly customer centric in that the needs and requirements of the customer must be communicated and transformed into goods and services that deliver value to the customer.

The *Marketing* function works closely with the customers in the target market in two major roles. First, the customers' needs/problems are identified and analyzed to define the products and services that customers would find valuable (innovation). Product management groups, for example, create detailed product specifications that are used to build the products, as well as product business plans that forecast demand and justify investments. Secondly, once the product is ready to go to market, marketing creates product literature, launches promotional campaigns, and supports sales efforts. The scale and tactics of the marketing function can vary widely depending on the size of the company and the industry segment of the target market.

The *Sales* function is represented graphically as a funnel indicating the filtering activity that typically happens when target customers are identified (candidates), qualified (prospects), and sold (buyers). Once again there are wide variances in the scale and timeframe associated with the sales function depending on the type of business and the purchase price of the product or service. The purchase of a McDonald's Happy Meal is highly automated, so Order Fulfillment takes only two or three minutes, whereas the purchase of a Caterpillar D9 tractor requires a highly-trained sales team with a months-long sales cycle.

The *Order Fulfillment Cycle*, also known as the "Order to Cash" cycle, is comprised of the value activities that start with the order from sales, pulling product from inventory, delivering the product to the customer, and then finishes with the receipt of payment (cash) from the customer.

The *Production Cycle* includes all the value activities associated with analysis, define, build, and validation of the product or service. At the mid-point of the Production Cycle, the materials or resources needed for the product or service are delivered by Procurement from suppliers in the supply chain. The procurement function is also represented as a filter because suppliers, and the goods and services they provide, are constantly being qualified, selected, and monitored based on cost, timeliness, and quality factors.

EXHIBIT 3-1. **The Dynamic Value Chain**

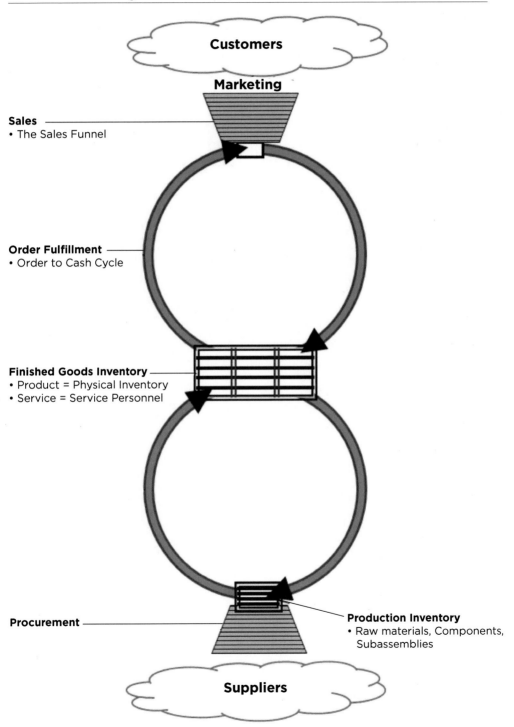

For companies, such as Caterpillar that sell discrete products, the Production Cycle is the manufacturing cycle. For existing products, the manufacturing cycle starts with the analysis of the current inventory position to arrive at a manufacturing capacity forecast, based on the current inventory position at the manufacturing plant and capacity forecasts at dealers. The forecast is then broken down into detailed manufacturing schedules, and material and resource plans in the define phase. Orders are placed by Procurement to their suppliers, who ship the materials to the plant to feed the build phase of production. The validation phase includes the quality management steps during manufacturing and any final product testing before it is placed into inventory or immediately shipped to dealers.

For companies that sell services, the Production Cycle involves the service delivery activities of analysis, define, build, and validation of the service deliverables (discrete documents for requirements, analysis, recommendations, etc.). If a management consulting service firm, for example, works with a customer on an assessment, they will plan the steps of the project and conduct requirements gathering and analysis to discover the existing situation and needs. During the define phase, the future state is defined with improvements to business outcomes or a solution to an identified problem. During the build phase, the service deliverables are created including presentations and documents that provide recommendations, workflow diagrams, solution definition, benefits, and financial justification for the changes. The assessment service deliverables are then quality checked, socialized, and presented to the management team to validate the solution. Frequently, there are multiple review cycles and adjustments to complete the final deliverable, which is then accepted and paid for by the customer through the second half of the Order Fulfillment Cycle.

Procurement manages the suppliers in the supply network that provide the raw materials, components, and service resources needed in the Production Cycle to produce the goods and services. Procurement utilizes a filtering approach similar to the sales funnel to evaluate and select suppliers that match the business goals to minimize cost while delivering the materials, components, and resources according to quality standards and established delivery timetables. Intensive communication between suppliers and procurement is required to manage the continuous flow of materials and resources to avoid supply outages and reduce work in progress inventory.

EXHIBIT 3-2. **Dynamic Value Chain Diagram with Process, People and Technology**

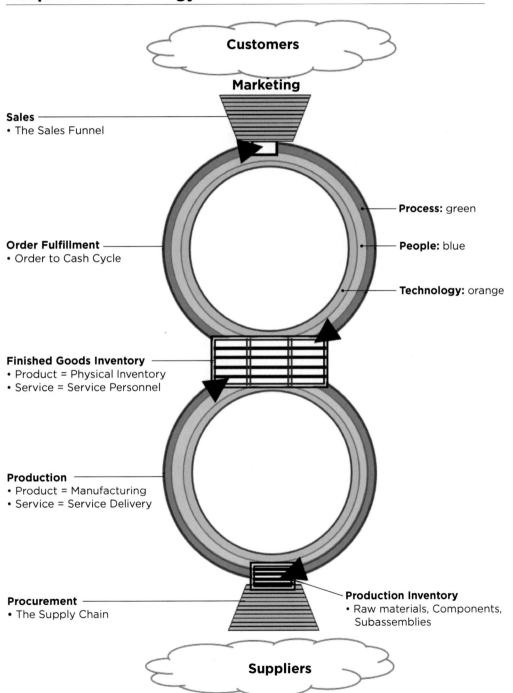

3.2 **Visualizing Process, People, and Technology of the Dynamic Value Chain**

The Dynamic Value Chain can be expanded to illustrate the relationship between the value processes, the people directly involved in the processes, and the technology/information systems that support the people and the processes. Exhibit 3-2, on the previous page, shows the layering of process, people, and technology for the two major Dynamic Value Chain cycles.

The marketing, sales, inventory, and procurement functions also have process, people, and technology elements to achieve their departmental objectives. For detailed analysis of the value-added business operations, the process, people, and technology elements for each functional area can be captured and mapped to the Dynamic Value Chain. As we will see in Chapter 10, optimizing the value activities of the business operation will focus on specific sections of the Dynamic Value Chain for tuning and improvement of overall business outcomes.

CHAPTER 4

Elements of the Dynamic Value Chain

4.1 The Customer

A value chain always starts with the customer and their needs or problems. Above all it is the customer's needs and problems that drive them to purchase a product or service, especially if there is a critical, time sensitive need associated with the purchase. Value is defined by the customer's desire to buy the product or service, including the price and a set of subjective factors. These subjective factors are expressed as benefits that include functionality, performance, reliability, aesthetics, customization, self-esteem, timeliness/convenience, and brand recognition. The customer seeks a "best fit" scenario between the requirements to satisfy their need and the perceived value of the goods or service (see section 8.1 for detail).

Customers are grouped into target markets that a business can serve, typically aligned with geographic areas. Retail businesses, for example, focus on local markets where customers travel a short distance and are influenced by retail store branding and signage. Larger industrial businesses, on the other hand, define their geographic markets on a much larger scale by city, state, nation, or global markets. Each target market can have unique customer requirements and related value definitions depending on economic, social, political, and cultural factors.

4.2 Marketing and Sales

Marketing contains two primary functions relative to the value chain approach: innovation of new goods and services, and go to market (GTM) activities for existing goods and services. The innovation process for creating new products and services is treated as a special version of the Dynamic Value Chain, because it is comprised of the value activities required to add new product offerings into inventory or new service offerings into the service catalog. Marketing seeks to combine an in-depth understanding of the requirements of targeted customer needs and problems with the product or service capabilities that produce benefits that are attractive to prospective buyers. Value is increased when marketing does a superior job of understanding the customer's needs and problems, and then specifies a product or service that meets those needs or solves the problem at an affordable price point. This will be addressed in more detail in Chapter 8, where we present ways to optimize the business for value creation and competitive advantage.

The GTM activities of the marketing function support the sales and distribution channels of the existing goods and services. In companies with high volume sales, such as consumer goods, food, and retail franchises, marketing serves to build a brand that large market sectors recognize. In companies with expensive products and services, marketing becomes more directly involved in the sales value activities in the following ways:

- Develops sales collateral to help the sales organization present the feature/benefit relationship

- Delivers various types of sales-lead generation activities, such as webinars, summits, conferences, and tradeshow events to identify and qualify sales prospects

- Establishes and maintains partnerships with compatible organizations that expand the sales function through distribution channels

There is a saying that "Sales makes the world go around," which is true in that the sales function brings in the orders that drives the purchasing/consumption of material goods and services, which in turn drives global economies. Clearly, sales personnel provide value by assisting the customer in the selection and buying process to match their requirements with the right goods and services to satisfy their need or solve a critical problem.

The concept of the sales function as a funnel was attributed to E. St. Elmo Lewis[1] when the phases of sales activities were established as *Attention, Interest,*

Desire, and *Action* (AIDA). Later *Satisfaction* was added to indicate that a customer had realized the value of the offering. These phases track the stages where individuals or businesses move through the sales process to buy a company's goods or services, and finally to the satisfaction stage where the customer has realized the benefits after implementation. The individuals or businesses who choose to buy from a competitor or decide not to buy at all, exit the funnel at various points in time, or loop back and reenter the funnel at a later time.

EXHIBIT 4.1. **The Sales Funnel**

The sales personnel educate the customer as they gain understanding of the goods or services, and move through the purchasing process. At a retail store, sales personnel help the customer find the product they are seeking, answer questions about the features of the product, and make the purchase transaction at the cash register. For larger, more complex purchases, a sales team of account managers, system engineers, lawyers, and sales managers may be required to work with multiple individuals in a customer's business to complete a transaction.

For the purposes of the Dynamic Value Chain, the sales funnel is a filtering mechanism. At the top of the funnel, there are *candidates* within the target market who have identified a need or problem (attention) and are interested in finding an appropriate goods or services. A candidate becomes a *lead* when the individual or business expresses interest to the seller about their particular goods or services. The lead becomes a *qualified prospect* once the sales person has worked with the customer to discuss their needs, product/service capabilities, solution fit, and purchasing plans (timing, process, approval). Finally, the qualified prospect becomes a *buyer* when the customer takes action through detailed discussions of price, terms and conditions, and implementation plans, ultimately leading to a purchase order.

The timeline and corresponding investment in the sales funnel varies dramatically by the size of the sales deal as illustrated below in Exhibit 4.2. The range of sales transactions start at the low end with on-line transactions for cell phone apps that occur in seconds, continues through retail transactions in minutes, to commercial and industrial transactions that take weeks or months, and finally reaches very large scale purchases in large industrial or government purchases that can take years to complete.

EXHIBIT 4-2. **Cost and Time of Sales by Size of Sales Deal**

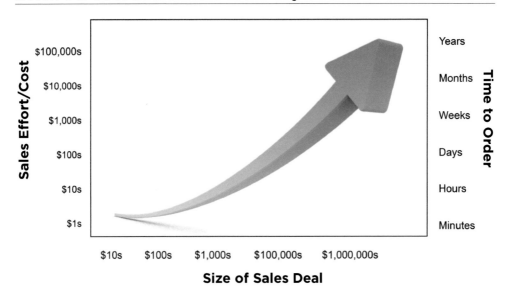

4.3 Inventory

In the Dynamic Value Chain, the Inventory element represents the existing goods or services that the enterprise has available for sale. In some businesses, the inventory includes the physical goods, but in other businesses the inventory of offerings is listed in a catalog and does not physically reside anywhere.

In a grocery or retail store, for example, the goods for sale are displayed on the shelves for customers to see, touch, and smell. They select the goods they desire and take them to the cash register to purchase them. The inventory would include the goods on the shelves and the items in storage at the rear of the store.

In a consulting service business, there is no physical inventory, so a service catalog is provided that lists the consulting services for sale. Services that are provided on a frequent basis are evolved into standard services in the catalog with fixed prices. Custom services are provided to meet non-standard customer requirements as specified in a service contract or statement of work (SOW). Considerably more work is involved in the sales cycle to create the SOW and associated price estimate for custom services on a fixed or time-and-material basis. Pricing strategies typically are complex with numerous factors to account for consultant skill levels, project management activities, risk mitigation, and contingency factors. In either case, the service deliverables (documents, presentations, data, and other service artifacts) are developed during the project (Production Cycle) and placed into inventory for customer delivery once completed.

The Dynamic Value Chain of a technical support group contains another interesting use of inventory. The customer contacts the help desk with a problem that needs attention. The help desk technician explores the problem with the customer to discover the details of the issue. She can then search a knowledge database (inventory) of documented problem/solution matches to find a potential solution for the customer. The larger and more accurate the knowledge database, the faster the technician can deliver the solution to the customer.

4.4 Order Fulfillment Cycle

The Order Fulfillment Cycle, also referred to as the order to cash cycle, is the portion of the value chain that starts with the receipt of the order from sales, follows the series of steps that pull the goods and services from inventory, delivers it to the customer, and ends with the receipt of payment for the goods and services. This value activity varies widely by industry and type of product or service, but in all cases the major driving factors are accuracy, quality, convenience, and timeliness. Did the customer receive what they ordered; did it meet their expectations for quality; was it easy to purchase; and did it arrive within the promised timeframe.

EXHIBIT 4-3. **The Order Fulfillment Cycle**

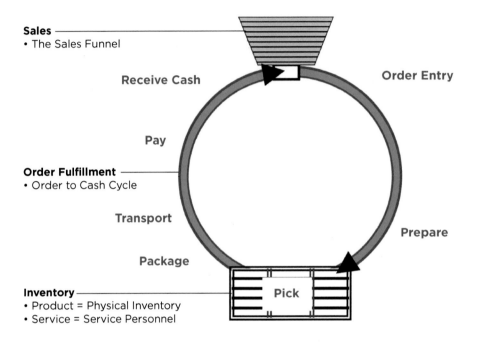

The Order Fulfillment Cycle has several stages as the order is processed, including review, prepare, pick, package, transport, pay and receive cash. The final output of the Order Fulfillment Cycle is the cash payment for the goods and services delivered to the customer. A straightforward example would be a manufacturing firm that produces products that are placed into an inventory for sale. The order from sales is entered into the order entry system, translated into a pick slip, and then reviewed by the warehouse personnel. They then go to the shelves, pick the specific products on the pick slip utilizing a bar code scanner, and then package the goods for shipment to the customer. Within the financial system an invoice is generated, the accounts receivable system is updated that a payment is due, and the invoice is sent to the customer's account payable department. The customer processes the invoice and sends the payment to the manufacturing firm, hopefully within the agreed upon payment terms, i.e. net

30 days. The accounts receivable department receives the payment and cashes the check, posting it into the financial system general ledger.

In the example of a retail store, the customer is much more involved in the Order Fulfillment Cycle, resulting in a much faster and simpler process that is more convenient for the customer. The customer enters the store, possibly just to look around, and then spots an attractive product that grabs her attention. She rapidly moves through the interest and desire steps of the AIDA sales cycle, sometimes with the help of a sales assistant who answers the customer's questions.

Once the customer decides to buy the product, she picks it from the shelf herself and takes it to the cash register (transport) and then pays for it in cash or with a credit card transaction. Since there is no order created in this streamlined process, the Order Fulfillment Cycle happens within a few minutes after the customer decides to purchase the product. The point of sales system registers the transaction, and later the transaction is communicated to the financial system to be posted as cash received.

4.5 **The Production Cycle**

The Production Cycle is the process by which the goods and services are created. As the Order Fulfillment Cycle is pulling goods and services from inventory, the Production Cycle is replenishing them back into inventory. In the case of discrete products, this is the manufacturing process, whereas in service businesses this is the process by which the service deliverables are created.

The Production Cycle includes four major stages: analyze, define, build, and validate. Depending on the industry, the terminology for these stages is different, but conceptually they are the same.

Production Cycle for Manufacturing

In the production of existing products, the goal is to produce the appropriate quantity of products to match the flow of orders in the Order Fulfillment Cycle. The analyze stage includes reviewing inventory positions, sales forecasts, and production schedules. A shop order is defined to meet the requirements from the analyze phase, and then materials are ordered from suppliers on a schedule that matches the build stage on the manufacturing floor. Finally, the products are validated through quality control and released to inventory. The Order Fulfillment Cycle then takes over, and picks the products from inventory, packages them, and ships them out to the customer.

EXHIBIT 4-4. **The Production Cycle**

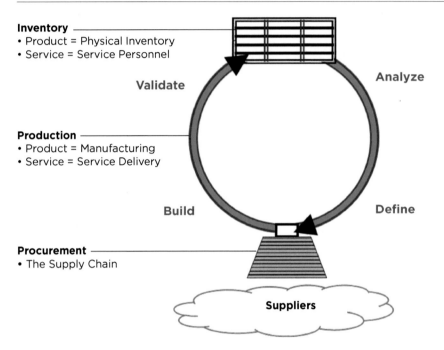

In some industries, there is an interesting dynamic between the Production Cycle and the Order Fulfillment Cycle. A tight interlock of the Order Fulfillment Cycle and Production Cycle occurs in cases where there is no finished goods inventory available to the Order Fulfillment Cycle, as is the case when a custom good or service deliverable is built, such as make-to-order manufacturing, the baking industry, or professional service firms. The custom product is placed briefly into finished goods inventory until it can be packaged for delivery to the customer.

Changes to the Production Cycle due to Innovation

When new products or services are needed, the Production Cycle becomes an innovation cycle to develop, build, and test the new innovations. The analysis stage focuses on the problems/needs of the customer, typically with input from product marketing and sales. The specific features driven by the customer's needs are then used to design a new product, complete with design documentation. Product forecasts, manufacturing capacity planning, and financial analysis are used to justify the new product concept to executive management. Process engineering activities define the new manufacturing processes and plant layout activities define the facility and physical arrangement of the manufacturing equipment.

Once the go ahead has been given, equipment and materials are ordered from suppliers and the build stage is conducted, frequently utilizing limited production runs or prototyping. The new product is validated through quality control and frequently delivered to select customers for short-term trials, i.e. focus groups or beta customers in the software industry. Depending on the feedback from the validation phase, additional test runs may be conducted, the product could be shelved, or it moves into full production.

4.6 **The Procurement Function**

In the Dynamic Value Chain, the procurement function is represented as a funnel, similar to the sales funnel. The procurement department works with many suppliers to evaluate the price, availability, technical specifications, and quality of their offerings. In this case, the procurement group is the customer and the suppliers are vying to sell their goods and services in a competitive environment.

EXHIBIT 4-5. **The Procurement Function**

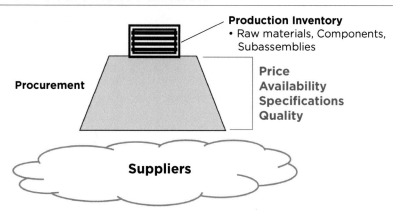

There is a filtering process involved in the procurement process that includes the selection of vendors to provide the raw materials, components, subassemblies, and services needed for production. In addition, there is a quality review filter (inspection) to evaluate incoming materials from established vendors, and reject those items that do not meet the established standards.

Procurement issues orders to the suppliers that are processed through their own Order Fulfillment Cycle. The goal of procurement is to manage the complex array of vendors and inbound materials in the supply chain to attain a consistent, dependable flow of materials to the Production Cycle while minimizing the cost of those materials to the company. In manufacturing companies, once the materials are received at the facility, they may be stored before being transported to the factory floor. There has been significant effort in manufacturing companies to work toward just-in-time supply chains to minimize inventories and corresponding carrying costs.

When considering procurement related to services, there are myriad ways to acquire human resources to perform the services in the Production Cycle:

- Full-time employees can be recruited and hired to join the company

- Independent service providers (sole practitioners/1099) can be hired for a period of time

- Resources from a staffing company can be added under a service contract for a period of time

- A subcontracting company can provide resources via a Statement of Work contract to deliver a portion of a project under the supervision of the company's project manager.

These resources would then be applied to the Production Cycle on a temporary or full-time basis.

CHAPTER 5

Value Chain Operational Models for Production Strategies

THERE ARE SEVERAL WELL-ESTABLISHED OPERATIONAL MODELS that support the specific production strategy of the business. These operational models are implemented to meet the needs of the business's target market with a focus on lead time and product customization. Four major operational models are: Make to Stock, Make to Order, Assemble to Order, and Engineer to Order. Exhibit 5-1 highlights the variety of customer lead times and customization for the operational models.

EXHIBIT 5-1. **Operational Models for Production Strategy**

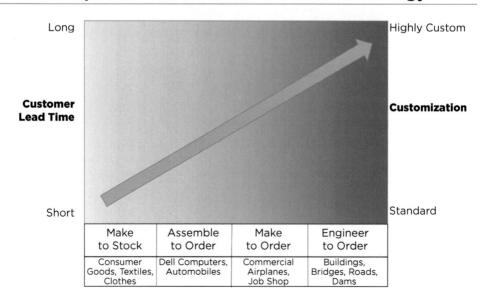

	Make to Stock	Assemble to Order	Make to Order	Engineer to Order
	Consumer Goods, Textiles, Clothes	Dell Computers, Automobiles	Commercial Airplanes, Job Shop	Buildings, Bridges, Roads, Dams

In the following sections, we will explore these operational models utilizing the Dynamic Value Chain framework to define the specific sequence of value-enhancing activities for each type of operational model.

5.1 **Make to Stock Model**

The *Make to Stock* model has been a dominant manufacturing practice since before the industrial revolution. A shoe cobbler in a nineteenth century town, for example, might build a set of popular shoes and place some in his store window. If the shoe remained popular, he would make these shoes in several sizes and put them in inventory. Products are manufactured and placed into an inventory for rapid picking and shipping to customers with minimal lead time.

This is a "push" approach to provide products to the market based on demand forecasting. The key elements of this model are a high-speed Order Fulfillment Cycle to deliver the goods and services rapidly, and a separate manufacturing cycle that is being driven continuously or in batches by automated manufacturing equipment and conveyor systems.

EXHIBIT 5-3. **Plastic Enclosure Continuous Manufacturing**

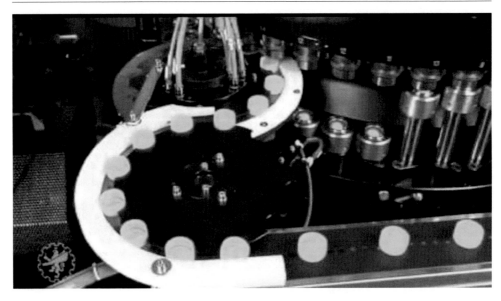

EXHIBIT 5-2. **Make to Stock Dynamic Value Chain**

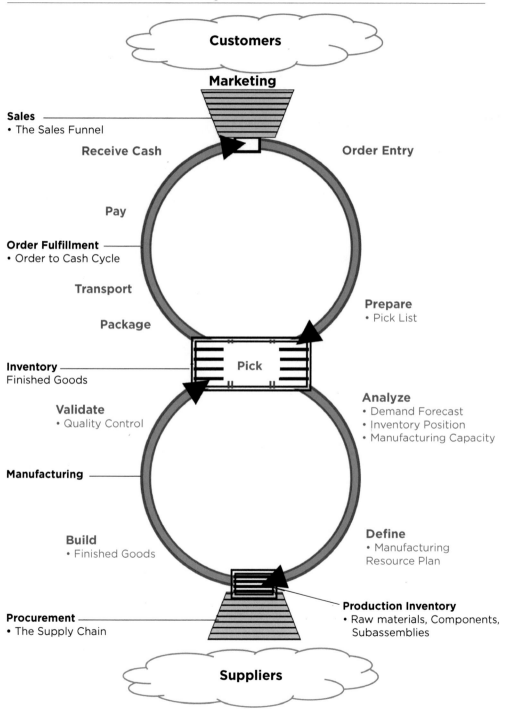

Customers

Marketing

Sales
• The Sales Funnel

Receive Cash   Order Entry

Pay

Order Fulfillment
• Order to Cash Cycle

Transport

Package   **Prepare**
                           • Pick List

Inventory
Finished Goods   **Pick**

                      Analyze
Validate   • Demand Forecast
• Quality Control   • Inventory Position
                      • Manufacturing Capacity

Manufacturing

Build   **Define**
• Finished Goods   • Manufacturing
                      Resource Plan

                      Production Inventory
Procurement   • Raw materials, Components,
• The Supply Chain   Subassemblies

Suppliers

A strong demand forecasting system is critical to avoid under producing (stock outages) or over producing (excess inventory, carrying charges, and financial write-offs). The Enterprise Resource Scheduling (ERP) application portfolios from SAP, Oracle, Microsoft, Netsuite, and others are needed to create a high-speed process and information network that closely integrates the sales, order fulfillment, manufacturing, and supply chain functions. Products provided by Make to Stock companies are typically consumer goods that are simple to produce, manufactured in large volumes, and are in high demand with little customization required.

There is a trend for companies to move from Make to Stock toward Make to Order when the customers require more customization to meet their specific requirements. Some companies, such as Nike, have incorporated *mass customization to* allow their customers to order variations to the standard product that are produced in a large-scale, Make to Stock manufacturing process. The NIKEiD program provides an on-line ordering capability with nine options for custom colors and graphics that a customer can select to create a one-of-a-kind athletic shoe.

5.2 Make to Order Model

The Make to Order model provides more customized goods and services with longer lead times than the Make to Stock model. The manufacturing cycle does not begin until the order has been received. This is a "pull" approach where manufacturing and the associated supply chain are driven by the actual sales demand of received orders. A key characteristic of the Make to Order model is the lack of finished goods inventory due to the custom nature of the manufacturing cycle. As orders are received from sales, they are entered into the order entry system, but there is no finished good inventory to be picked and shipped to the customer at this point, so the value chain process moves directly to the Production Cycle's analysis step where a manufacturing engineer reviews the customer requirements.

EXHIBIT 5-4. **Make to Order Dynamic Value Chain**

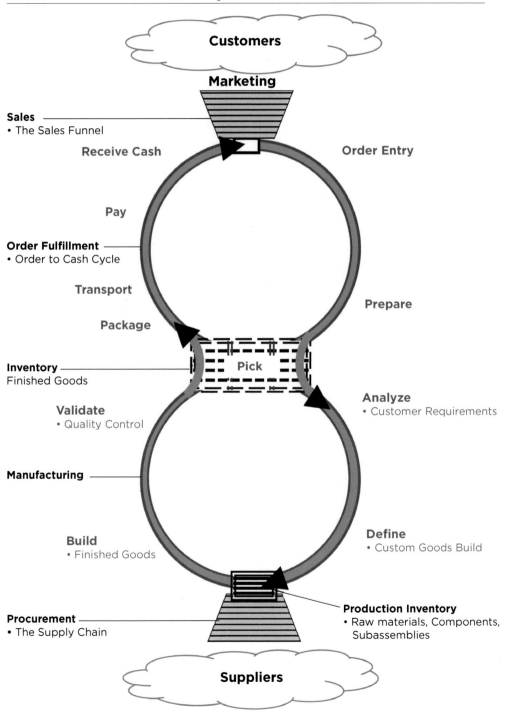

A manufacturing work order is then defined to utilize an existing manufacturing process or a custom process outlining the manufacturing steps needed to produce the product. These manufacturing work orders may call out small-run batches or individual product creation typical of *job shops* where the product is machined through a series of process steps in various work centers across the shop floor. A job shop is frequently a small- to medium-size operation providing machined metal or plastic parts to a larger manufacturer.

The shop floor is organized by grouping machines of similar types, and workers are trained to operate several of these machines to be able to manufacturer a variety of products.

EXHIBIT 5-5. **Metal Parts Manufacturing Job Shop**

With permission from Major Tool & Machine, Inc.

Following defined process workflows, the product moves from area to area through a series of activities at the specialized machines.

EXHIBIT 5-6. **Typical Job Shop Floor Plan with Production Workflow Along the Red Lines**

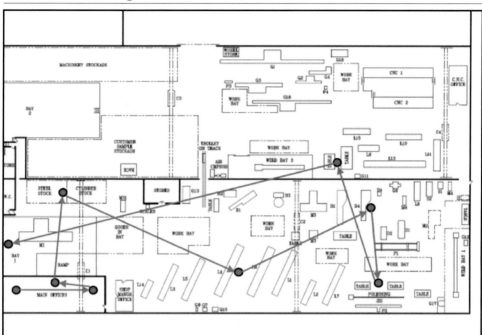

Suppliers who are partnering with Make to Order companies are being asked to deliver their raw materials, components, and subassemblies in a Just in Time timeframe to reduce production inventories and related carrying costs. The procurement department and the associated supply chain management information systems become strategic as they focus on reducing the delivery time and increasing the reliable availability of quality components for production.

Once quality control testing has been completed to validate that the product meets the customer's custom specification, the Production Cycle is complete and the Make to Order parts are ready to be packaged and sent to the customer. This bypasses finished goods inventory again, unless products of a batch order need to be stored temporarily, while the batch process is being completed, so that all the products are available for a single shipment.

5.3 **Assemble to Order Model**

The Assemble to Order model is similar to the Make to Order model in that work does not start until the order is received from sales. The customer receives a customized product with a shorter lead time than Make to Order. The difference here is that there is no creation of products via material transformation steps, but only assembly (and testing) of pre-made components and subassemblies. The Production Cycle is usually faster because the product is manufactured by assembling standard components. The production inventory and supply chain are important elements to ensure that there is an adequate supply of components or subassemblies available to meet production demands.

5.4 **Engineer to Order Model**

The Engineer to Order model is another variation on the Make to Order model, except in this case some of the components or the entire product must be defined and created to meet the customer requirements as specified in the order or service contract. Customer lead times are typically long due to the custom design cycle (production) time.

Many automotive suppliers, for example, design and build custom parts based on specifications and drawings from their partner automotive companies using an Engineer to Order approach. This can take time to create engineering drawings from the specifications, review them with the customer, define a custom manufacturing process, and then use specialized Numerical Control machines to create the product using computerized instructions to machine the part from a block of metal.

In addition, this type of value chain model includes architecture, engineering, and consulting firms who build buildings, dams, bridges, roads, and other solutions over extended periods of time. Let's follow an example of an architectural firm designing a commercial office building. The value chain process starts in the sales cycle with extensive requirements-gathering and definition of the design concept. Initial estimates are developed to provide the customer with a budgetary estimate of the building construction cost. Typically, the winning architecture firm

EXHIBIT 5-7. **Assemble to Order Dynamic Value Chain**

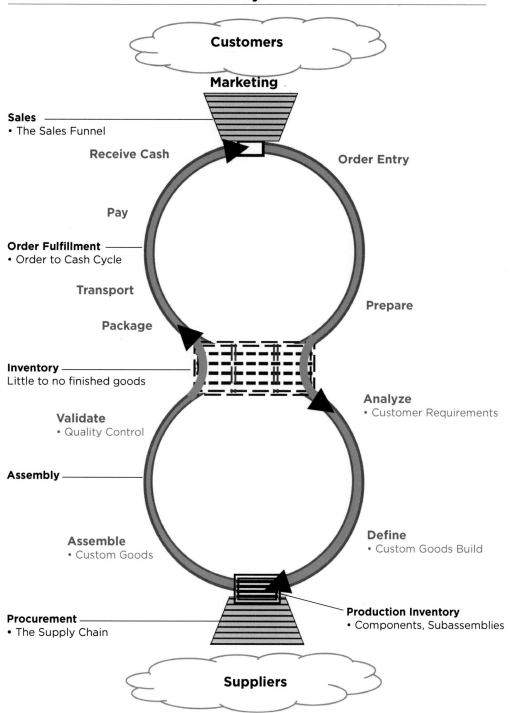

Customers

Marketing

Sales
• The Sales Funnel

Receive Cash

Order Entry

Pay

Order Fulfillment
• Order to Cash Cycle

Transport

Prepare

Package

Inventory
Little to no finished goods

Analyze
• Customer Requirements

Validate
• Quality Control

Assembly

Assemble
• Custom Goods

Define
• Custom Goods Build

Procurement
• The Supply Chain

Production Inventory
• Components, Subassemblies

Suppliers

EXHIBIT 5-8. **Engineer to Order Dynamic Value Chain**

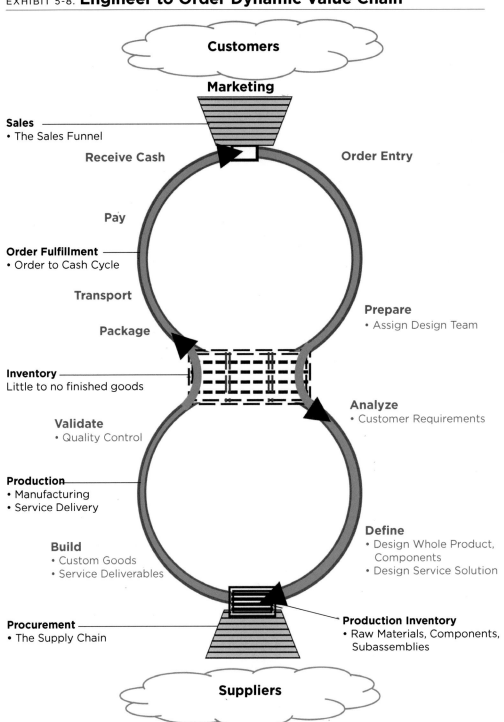

is selected through competitive bidding with a proposal, design models, and extensive contract negotiation.

The winning firm receives a signed contract and purchase order to proceed with the design. As the Order Fulfillment Cycle begins, the contract is reviewed by the team leader and a design team of architects, draftspersons, project manager, and support personnel to understand the scope of work and deliverables called out in the contract. The design team conducts a series of pre-engagement meetings (prepare) to establish roles and responsibilities, develops a project schedule, and finalizes the detailed customer requirements with the customer. The team launches the project in a kick-off meeting by reviewing the project objectives, customer requirements, project plan, and deliverable list with the customer.

As the Order Fulfillment Cycle reaches the inventory, there are no completed service deliverables available, since the design documents and specifications are created on a custom basis for each customer. Most firms have standard design templates available as a starting point for the deliverables, so these are utilized to begin the deliverable creation process. At this point, the value chain process enters the Production Cycle to create the custom design deliverables, through a series of project phases—Programming, Schematic Design, Design Development, Construction Documents, and Construction Administration documents. Each phase generates design deliverables that once completed, are placed in the document inventory and completes a cycle for each round of deliverables, as milestones on the overall project plan.

At that point the Order Fulfillment Cycle can continue as copies of the design documents (blueprints and specification documents) are packaged and transported to the customer and construction contractors where appropriate. The customer is sent an invoice as design documents are completed or milestones are reached, which they pay according to their contractual payment terms. This cycle of production spins numerous times as each service deliverable is completed and placed into inventory. The Order Fulfillment Cycle completes its rotation to transport and receive payment for each deliverable or milestone, after it has been created and checked into inventory.

5.5 **Summary**

The Dynamic Value Chains presented in this chapter cover the major standard operation models. Exhibit 5-9 summarizes the key features of each of these Dynamic Value Chains.

EXHIBIT 5-9. **Summary of Production Dynamic Value Chains**

	Make To Stock	Assemble To Order	Make To Order	Engineer To Order
Sales Orders	• Push to Market • Demand Forecast	• Pull based on Orders • Custom Configuration	• Pull based on Orders • Custom Specification	• Pull based on Contract • Statement of Work
Product Variety Customization	Low	Medium	High	Very High
Production Workflow	Continuous Process	Assembly Line	Product Moves to Work Centers	Extensive Design Cycle Materials to Build Site
Wait Time between Steps	Very Low	Low	Medium	High

CHAPTER 6

Multiple Value Chains within One Company

In Michael Porter's original Value Chain model, there is one value chain within a company with primary functions that include inbound logistics, operations, outbound logistics, sales and marketing, and service. Since a company can provide value to customers via multiple types of offerings, a company may contain one or multiple value-added business segments, each with their own unique value chain. A value-added business segment becomes unique when the related functional elements are combined in distinct ways to deliver value to the customer.

Key Principal: A company can have one to many value chains that deliver value offerings to their client each with their own discrete workflows and personnel.

6.1 Multiple Value Chains Example

A technology product vendor, such as IBM, HP, Oracle, or EMC, for example, has multiple value-added business segments that contain unique combinations of processes, people, and information systems to deliver the total business solution to the customer.

1. Providing the product offering—physical hardware or software licenses to their customers

2. Providing professional services to consult, define, install, and customize the technology in the customer's environment

3. Providing technical support after the implementation of the systems via a help desk

The technology vendor works closely with the customer to select and deliver an appropriate set of hardware and software in the first value added business segment. The customer is billed at the time of shipment of the goods per a product quote and a master sales agreement. The second value added business segment provides a service project with a separate master service agreement, unique personnel (solution architects, consultants, and project managers), and separate information systems to estimate work effort, track billable hours during the project, and then bill the customer in increments (monthly or milestone billing) over the duration of the project. Finally, the customer calls the support organization help desk to answer technical problems, and to discuss maintenance with another group of technical specialists who are trained on customer support techniques and utilize help ticket and knowledge base systems (inventory of technical issues and solutions).

EXHIBIT 6-1. **Multiple Dynamic Value Chains**

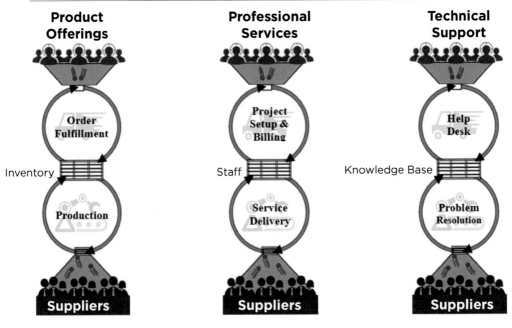

The technology vendor has a marketing and sales organization that identifies prospects and then works closely with the potential customer to select an appropriate set of hardware and software in the first value chain. A proposal and a product quote are provided and then once accepted, an internal order is created to complete the order fulfillment cycle. The products are selected from inventory, shipped to the customer location, and an invoice is sent to the customer for the purchase.

The second value chain provides a professional service project to implement or upgrade the hardware and software with a separate contract—the Statement of Work (SOW). The product sales team (or separate service sales team) relies heavily on the involvement of key service experts who define the service project in close collaboration with the customer. The SOW is signed and then becomes the order that is used to complete the Order Fulfillment Cycle. Prior to then project start, resources are allocated to the project from available professional services staff (inventory). The unique project team personnel (solution architects, consultants, and project managers) work with customer personnel to create specific work products to deliver the service. The customer is billed incrementally (weekly, monthly, or per work product delivery) over the duration of the project.

Finally, the technical support value chain occurs when the customer calls the support organization help desk to answer technical problems. A trouble ticket is opened as the order that is used to complete the problem/solution cycle. The problem is researched within a knowledge base—inventory of solutions to technical issues—or knowledge from other technical specialists who are trained on customer support techniques. If technical issues cannot be solved by first-tier technical specialists, the problem resolution cycle includes escalation to tier two and tier three advanced specialists with specialized knowledge. The cost to the customer is either included in the original product sales as a line item or sold by maintenance sales personnel.

This example illustrates that a firm can have more than one distinctive value chain when there are separate personnel, processes, and information systems to deliver value to the customer. Each has unique value propositions (and related competitive strategy) that meet the needs of the target market.

6.2 **The Innovation Value Chain Found in All Companies**

As multiple value chains are considered within companies, it becomes clear that innovation is a distinct value chain in nearly all businesses. The strength and presence of the innovation value chain varies by company, growing from nearly non-existent to a strategic foundation for the company (Corning, Apple, Google, 3M, Microsoft, Lilly, GM). Innovation is typically considered as something inherent—woven into the fabric of the business. But in most firms, it can be identified as its own distinct value chain with focused projects and frequently, dedicated people, processes, facilities, and information systems.

Key Principal: Every company has an innovation value chain that is used to create and test new offerings. The innovation value chain becomes the key to a product excellence competitive strategy in companies such as 3M, Apple, and Corning.

Innovation value chains will draw from other departmental groups, but the goal of innovation drives the process to create new goods and services that are valued by customers. Innovative ideas frequently come from in-depth customer interaction in sales or product marketing. Requirements are gathered and analyzed, and a selection process is used (the funnel) to determine the best ideas to pursue. Once the innovation process moves into the solution development cycle, work may be conducted in a research and development (R&D) facility or an engineering center. In a manufacturing company, prototypes are built and tested, now using new techniques such as 3D printing. Further testing in the manufacturing facility involves special production runs to work out procedures and workflows that later will become the final production process. As the final product and manufacturing process is nearing completion, the Order Fulfillment Cycle reaches the launch stage with marketing campaigns and announcements.

EXHIBIT 6-2. **The Innovation Value Chain**

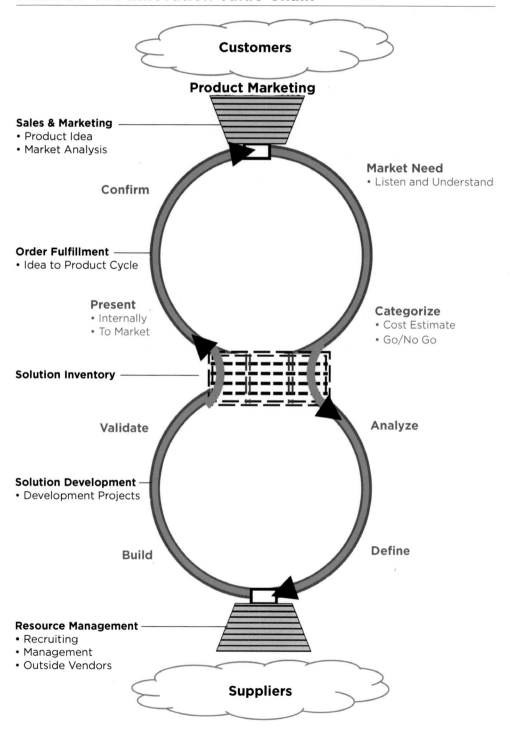

Customers

Product Marketing

Sales & Marketing
• Product Idea
• Market Analysis

Market Need
• Listen and Understand

Confirm

Order Fulfillment
• Idea to Product Cycle

Present
• Internally
• To Market

Categorize
• Cost Estimate
• Go/No Go

Solution Inventory

Validate

Analyze

Solution Development
• Development Projects

Build

Define

Resource Management
• Recruiting
• Management
• Outside Vendors

Suppliers

CHAPTER 7

Distribution Channels and the Supply Chain

As business organizations evolved in the industrial age, companies grew in size and geographic reach. Advances in manufacturing and transportation of goods made it possible to produce products at higher volumes that could be sold to broader customer markets. The automobile industry, for example, evolved from custom built, small quantity production of automobiles in the late-nineteenth century to large-scale manufacturing in the twentieth century. The volume of automobile sales increased dramatically as the "horseless carriage" became an accepted mode of transportation, creating more and more pressure for the manufacturing facilities to increase production by opening new plants and developing innovation in the manufacturing process.

Although the concept of an assembly line had been used sporadically in the past, it was Ransom Olds of Olds Motor Company who is credited with the development of the automobile assembly line in 1901.[1] But his accomplishment was eclipsed when in 1913, Henry Ford launched the modern assembly line for the Model T that could produce a vehicle in 93 minutes.[2] With this dramatic increase in manufacturing speed, and the emergence of a massive market for automobiles, the sales function needed to expand beyond direct sales to distribution channels to provide local retail outlets in many U.S. cities.

The Ford distribution channel (dealer network) started slowly in 1903 when the first dealership was opened by William Hughson in San Francisco with 12 Model A cars.[3] James Couzens, an early Ford shareholder, expanded the dealer network to 450 agents by 1904. By 2003, there were 4,500 Ford dealers in the United States to meet the demand for sales and service of Ford cars and trucks.

A distribution channel provides a more cost-effective means of selling a high volume of products through dealer networks, retail stores, manufacturer representatives, or value-added resellers. Each producer designs a distribution channel that meets their specific requirements with three primary considerations: *efficiency* (getting products to retailers and consumers at the lowest cost), *effectiveness* (market coverage and quality of services provided), and *control* (ability to determine timing and focus of distribution efforts).[4] In the case of consumer goods, retail shops and dealer networks carry an inventory of products that customers can view, touch, smell, try on, test drive, etc.

With the advent of eCommerce in the 1990s, *online sales channels* created another evolution of distribution. Goods began to be sold via websites with a product catalog that contained pictures, descriptive information, pricing, and customer reviews about the product. Although eCommerce was originally touted as eliminating the physical store, many consumers still wanted an in-store shopping experience to physically evaluate certain products before they purchased. eCommerce sites have continued to grow to become an important channel for product sales in combination with physical stores (bricks and clicks).

As volume of product sales continues to climb, a high-volume distribution channel may be designed as a multistage distribution process including *distributors*—intermediary distribution centers that manage a large inventory in a regional warehouse to provide stock to local retailers/resellers. This multi-tier distribution structure involves the flow of goods from company to company, where each business takes ownership of the products as they are shipped to the next company in the chain. The following sections provide the value chain business models for retail, reseller, and distributors along with a high-level description of their business activities.

7.1 Retail Model

The retail model is built to provide a specific set of goods (clothes, shoes, electronics, groceries, etc.) to consumer customers where they can shop quickly and select the goods that meet their needs via a self-service Order Fulfillment Cycle. Retail stores can be individual boutiques with a select set of products in a shopping mall, department stores with numerous sections organized by product types

EXHIBIT 7-1. **Retail Dynamic Value Chain**

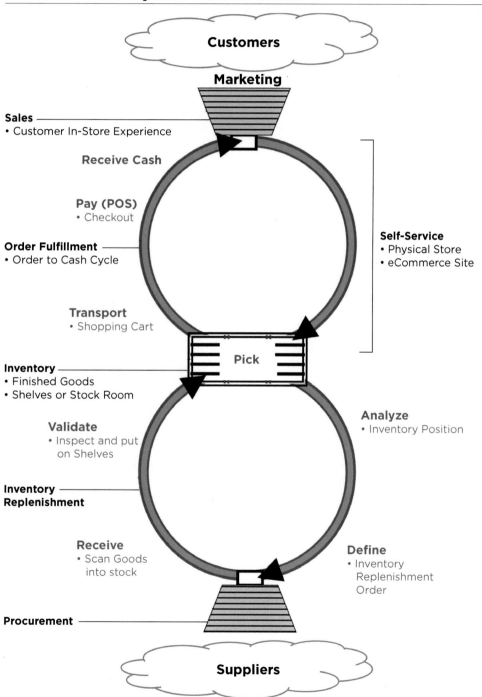

or brands, grocery stores, or big box stores that aggregate groceries, clothes, electronics, and home products in a warehouse-sized facility. Starting with their exposure to the products through marketing campaigns by the manufacturer, as well as the in-store shopping experience, customers proceed through the AIDA sales stages—attention, interest, desire, and action. A sales assistant is available to answer questions and assist with the purchase. Once the customer selects the product they want to buy, they transport the product in a shopping cart to the point of sale (cash registers or on-line checkout).

In retail business operations, the Order Fulfillment Cycle has been enhanced over the decades to be faster and more accurate to serve the customers' demands for faster delivery. Shopping and payment processes in shopping malls, grocery stores, fast food restaurants, and gas stations have all changed to accommodate a faster Order Fulfillment Cycle.

The Order Fulfillment Cycle of the grocery store, for example, has evolved over time depending on the needs of their customers. In an 1800s-general store, the customer would ask the clerk for the needed items. The clerk would go to the shelves and pick the items to bring to the front counter. The customer would then pay cash for their purchase at the cash register. Other customers waited until it was their turn to get their items. This was acceptable in a time when the pace of life was slower.

In 1916, Piggly Wiggly opened the first self-service grocery store in Memphis, TN, to allow customers to go to the shelves themselves to pick items to bring to the cash registers.[5] At the time, this approach was a breakthrough in grocery merchandising that reduced the number of store clerks and sped up the shopping experience.

Photo with permission from Piggly Wiggly

The grocery store continued to evolve into the supermarket where there is a vast array of products, many cash register lanes, self-checkout lanes, and high-speed cash and credit systems to expedite the checkout process.

The grocery Order Fulfillment Cycle continued to evolve along the lines of convenience and timeliness by businesses such as Peapod, founded in 1989 in Evanston, Illinois.[6] Peapod pioneered the on-line grocery business model providing customers with grocery shopping and delivery via a web-based catalog. Peapod grew slowly at first, hitting their one-millionth order nine years later due to the reluctance of customers to change their grocery buying habits. Today, Peapod has reached 23 million orders and enhanced their Order Fulfillment model by placing more than a hundred virtual grocery stores at commuter rail stations. A busy commuter can walk up to a billboard with pictures of grocery goods on shelves and scan a barcode with their smartphone to add items to their order that will be delivered to their home.

The Production Cycle in the retail model is an inventory replenishment cycle to keep the stockroom and display shelves properly stocked. The inventory is tracked with an inventory management system and managed by the store manager with the goal of maintaining adequate stock levels. This is a balance between avoiding "stock outs," where customers cannot immediately buy the product they are seeking, and "overstock," where inventory is not being sold, which increases inventory carrying costs. This balancing act to optimize stock levels is challenging due to myriad variations in buying trends, marketing programs, seasonal adjustments, weather, and economic situations. The store manager analyzes the inventory position on a regular basis and defines orders to the various suppliers and distributors who provide the goods for sale in the retail store. The bulk shipment of ordered goods is received at the loading dock and scanned into inventory using a radio frequency identification (RFID) barcode scanner. The individual products are inspected (validate), labeled with price tags, and placed on the shelf by stocking personnel.

7.2 **The Reseller Model**

A reseller business is a simpler value chain that includes product sourcing as its Production Cycle. The reseller typically does not carry a physical inventory and relies on the manufacturing business (or distributor) to ship the product directly to the reseller's customers (drop ship). Resellers are part of a larger distribution channel that provides the manufacturer with an expanded network

EXHIBIT 7-2. **Reseller Dynamic Value Chain**

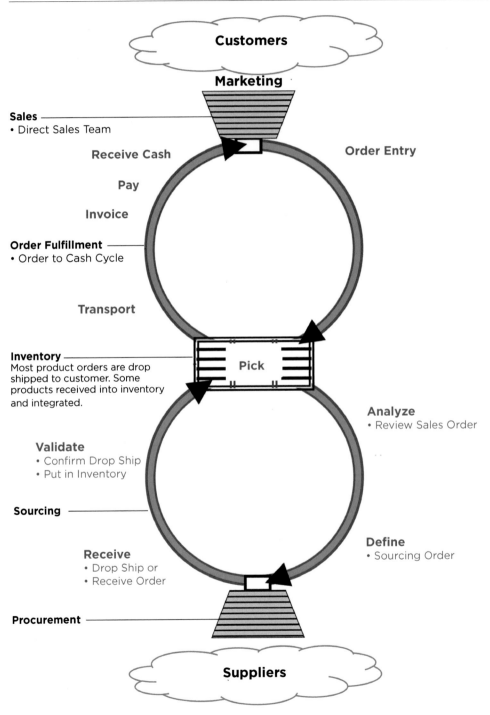

of sales outlets. Resellers can range from small home-based businesses that resell inexpensive consumer products through eBay, to larger value-added resellers (VARs) that provide the end customer with a local business that can implement and service a custom solution. Software companies and technology manufacturers, for example, establish VAR networks when their products have strong market acceptance and sales volumes grow beyond the capacity of their direct sales force.

The manufacturer conducts major marketing advertising and brand development to generate market pull for the goods and services through the reseller network. The reseller's marketing activities are focused on identifying local prospects, educating potential buyers about product features and benefits, and managing relationships with existing customers. Each reseller hires technical sales personnel including account managers and system engineers to work with prospects during a sales cycle that can last for days or months depending on the cost/complexity of the purchase and the size of the bureaucracy of the customer organization.

Many technology resellers specialize in one or more solution areas that combine multiple products and services to deliver a complete solution that meets the customer's specific requirements. During the sales cycle, system engineers and implementation consultants collaborate with the customer to design a viable, cost-effective solution. Some customers will define the solution requirements in a Request for Proposal (RFP) document that is provided to multiple competing companies to respond with their solution definition and pricing proposal.

Once a purchase order has been received by the reseller, it is entered into the order entry system. The reseller's procurement personnel then place an order to the technology manufacturer or distributor to ship the products directly to the customer's site. When a system is more complex with multiple hardware and software components, the products are shipped to the reseller for assembly and testing before final delivery to the customer site. Once the products have been shipped to the customer, the reseller invoices the customer for the products and the customer then has a defined number of days (net 30, 60, 90 days, etc.) to pay the invoice. The reseller's accounts receivable personnel track the outstanding payments, send reminders when payments are overdue, and post payments to the accounting system once they are received.

Since the reseller business model is notably simpler because they do not produce the products, resellers are perceived as having lower value-add. Customers, especially larger organizations with established purchasing departments, place their purchase requirements out for competitive bids to multiple resellers rather than single sourcing the purchase. This makes it even more difficult for a reseller to show value or establish a strong relationship with a customer. As a result, resellers are constantly looking for ways to add value to the pure product play. Resellers will apply one or more of the following tactics to show value and differentiate their business:

- Hold educational seminars on new products
- Bring together industry experts to share the latest trends with customers
- Create customer advisory councils, where customers network with peers and share their perspectives
- Provide frequent purchasing programs
- Specialize in a niche solution that is in demand in the marketplace
- Provide advisory and implementation services to properly set up and customize the solution

7.3 The Distributor Model

One strategy that accommodates large-scale product flow is a *two-tier distribution channel*. In this scenario, a distributor operates between the producer and the sales outlets (retailers, resellers, manufacturer representatives) that provide the goods for sale to consumers. A large producer may have several distributors and thousands of resellers or retail outlets across wide geographic or global regions. The distributors own large warehouse facilities to house significant inventories of goods from one or more producers. Their operations are streamlined to move massive quantities of goods in and out of inventory, and their business functions on very low gross profit margins.

To illustrate the distributor Dynamic Value Chain, let's look at the computer system distribution company, Access Graphics. They grew rapidly in the mid- to late-1990s as a major distributor for high-tech products such as Unix workstations, printers, plotters, and storage devices from multiple technology manufacturers. They sold to five thousand technology resellers across the U.S. and Canada that provided computer systems to engineering and information technology departments in medium- and large-size businesses. Access Graphics had two sales teams—an outside sales team responsible for the recruitment and relationships with regional resellers (customers) and an inside sales team that worked with the resellers daily to quote and place product orders. The inside sales team communicated product information that included technical specifications, configuration requirements, pricing, availability, and status of orders.

Access Graphics' business operations were built to handle the fast delivery requirements of the technology resellers and their end-user customers. The Order Fulfillment Cycle ran at an incredible rate. From the time that a reseller first contacted Access Graphics to discuss placing an order to the time that an order was shipped out the door at the warehouse was 24 hours for 65 percent of the orders, and 48 hours for 90 percent of the orders. In 1997, this represented $7M of goods shipped per day from two 100,000 square foot warehouses with total annual revenues exceeding a billion dollars.

The Production Cycle in the distributor value chain is an inventory replenishment cycle that involves analyzing the inventory position and placing orders with the manufacturing suppliers. The inventory replenishment cycle took two to three weeks to complete, so the procurement department, with multiple procurement managers analyzing their assigned product lines, paid close attention to the order flow and inventory positions to place timely orders to their suppliers. The procurement managers were tasked to avoid out of stock situations for high-volume products and reduce inventory carrying costs on low-volume products.

Distribution channels are typically driven by contractual agreements that provide guidelines for the margins that the distributors and resellers can make on their sales. Care is taken to reduce "low-ball selling" by resellers that want to book business by lowering prices below established guidelines, because that puts pricing pressure on all the resellers, and ultimately leads to less profit for all players. In the 1990s, Unix computer system resellers could make 12 to 18 percent gross profit on their product sales, with additional implementation services in the 30 to 45 percent gross profit range. Access Graphics on the other hand ran their high speed, efficient distribution business on 7 percent gross profit. With such a low-margin business, a great deal of attention was placed

EXHIBIT 7-3. **Distributor Dynamic Value Chain**

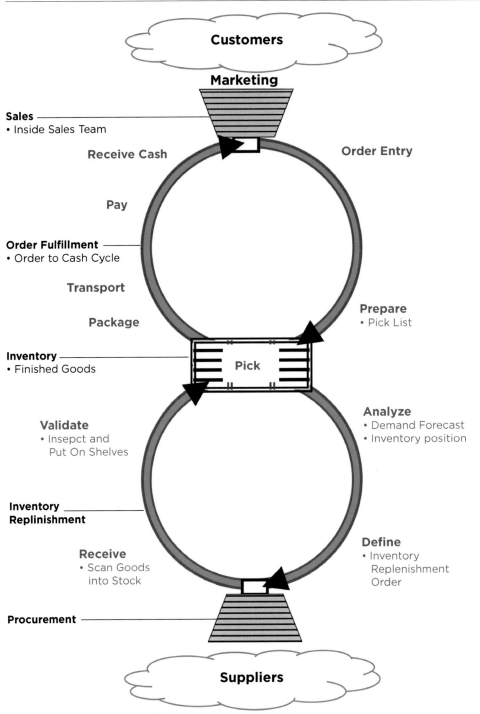

on the recruitment of new resellers to grow the volume of business that would provide the advantage of economies of scale.

Access Graphics provided additional value-add capabilities that were attractive to potential new computer system resellers. Each of these capabilities was established with their own personnel and operational processes, and therefore represents a set of value chains in tandem with the distributor's core business model. These ancillary value chains provided:

- Financing services—lines of credit so resellers could better manage their cash flow

- Technical support—tiered customer support to handle reseller technical issues

- Return material authorization (RMA) process—returning products for credit

- Packaged marketing programs—marketing programs and materials utilizing manufacturer incentives to extend resellers' marketing reach on a regional basis

- Consulting services network—access to technical consultants from a wide network of consulting firms to handle large or specialized consulting projects for the resellers' customers

The combination of an expanding computer systems market in the 1990s, an efficient core order fulfillment business, and the ancillary value chains enabled Access Graphics to recruit thousands of new resellers and grow revenues between 20 and 70 percent per year. Many of the new Access Graphics resellers transitioned from other computer distributors due to the total value package of services and capabilities that Access Graphics offered. This is an excellent example of a company that provides multiple value chains that are attractive to its customers and thus establish a competitive advantage that allows the company to grow.

A multi-stage distribution channel, combining the businesses of manufacturer, distributors, and retailers/resellers, becomes a complex network of companies working to efficiently deliver a large volume of products to the manufacturer's end customers. Exhibit 7-4 illustrates the network of value chains to deliver the manufacturer's products through an integrated two-tier distribution channel.

EXHIBIT 7-4. **The Two-Tier Distribution Channel Model**

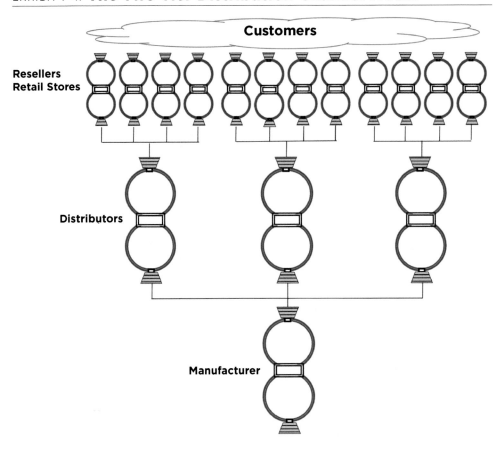

7.4 **Evolution of the Supplier Network**

As described in Chapter 4, the procurement function is the interface between the company and its suppliers. Procurement is responsible for the timely purchasing of raw materials, parts, and subassemblies needed for the production cycle. Procurement's mission is to manage the flow of production materials to keep the production process running smoothly with a focus on quality, cost, availability, and technical specifications. Procurement exerts control over their suppliers to optimize the mix of these four elements to meet the strategy of the company, i.e. low cost provider versus premium quality provider.

Supply-side purchasing has always been a part of a business, but the span and sophistication has evolved over time, especially as production and distribution grew in scale to accommodate the vast expansion of global markets in the twentieth century. In the late-nineteenth century, large corporations strove to actively control all their suppliers through *vertical integration* of the flow of raw materials and the supplier companies.

EXHIBIT 7-5. **The Supply Network Model**

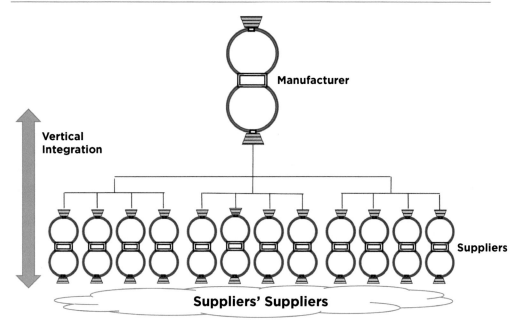

One of the greatest experiments in controlling the vertical integration of the supply side of manufacturing production was Henry Ford's grand vision of extending Ford's corporate umbrella to include the supply of the raw materials needed to produce a Ford Model A. As described in the Ford Rouge website,[7] the Rouge Factory (the Rouge) was a vast complex of 93 buildings with over 16 million square feet, measuring a mile and a half wide by more than a mile long located near the confluence of the Detroit and Rouge Rivers. Henry Ford's vision was to achieve total self-sufficiency by owning, operating, and managing all the resources and upstream production to build his automobiles. As he started his grand development, Ford owned vast holdings of land, coal mines, and even a rubber plantation in Brazil. In 1917 he started building the Rouge a section at a time, until 1927 when the Rouge supplied everything required to build the Model A automobile.

"There were ore docks, steel furnaces, coke ovens, rolling mills, glass furnaces, and plate-glass rollers. Buildings included a tire-making plant, stamping plant, engine casting plant, frame and assembly plant, transmission plant, radiator plant, tool and die plant, and at one time even a paper mill. A massive power plant produced enough electricity to light a city the size of nearby Detroit, and a soybean conversion plant turned soybeans into plastic auto parts. The Rouge had its own railroad with 100 miles of track and 16 locomotives. A scheduled bus network and 15 miles of paved roads kept everything and everyone on the move.

"It was a city without residents. At its peak in the 1930s, more than 100,000 people worked at the Rouge. To accommodate them required a multi-station fire department, a modern police force, a fully staffed hospital, and a maintenance crew 5,000 strong. One new car rolled off the line every 49 seconds. Each day, workers smelted more than 1,500 tons of iron and made 500 tons of glass, and every month 3,500 mop heads had to be replaced to keep the complex clean."

The Rouge has continued its production of automobile components to this day, albeit in a diminished capacity. After Henry Ford's death, the company began decentralizing the operations, and has sold off most of the supply side operations. Through the largest industrial revitalization effort in U.S. history and the support of the United Auto Workers union, the Rouge has emerged as The Rouge Center with 600 acres where Ford trucks are produced in the Dearborn Truck Plant.

Few companies have the single-minded leadership and financial resources of Henry Ford, but his vision of a consolidated and integrated supply network is indicative of the desire of most companies to control their suppliers and the flow of materials to optimize their production cycle. As the twentieth century progressed, the majority of manufacturing companies learned that it was better to diversify their enterprise of supplier businesses to focus on their core competencies.

7.5 **Evolution of Procurement and the Emergence of the Supply Chain**

By the 1970s, most companies evolved their procurement, forecasting, production, transportation, and warehousing in separate vertical functions with poor cross-communication and integration. Due to the different goals and compensation incentives of these functions, counter-productive outcomes can result. When excessive emphasis is placed on acquiring the lowest-cost parts in the procurement department, the cost of production can increase dramatically due to rework of low-quality parts. The company may even have to initiate recalls once the final product has been delivered to the marketplace, which are not only expensive, but can damage their reputation as evidenced recently by General Motors' numerous recalls.

Procurement focused on the inbound supply activities to the point of production and became known as *material management*, while the outbound activities after the production of the goods were called *physical distribution*. Then in the 1980s, some corporations found advantages in managing a broader perspective of their internal operations by adopting the concept of *integrated business logistics* that spanned the sourcing, production, and delivering of products.[8] This was the beginning of the *supply chain* concept.

Starting in the late 1980s and early '90s, many large companies began to look outside of their internal operations at both upstream (supply network) and downstream (sales and distribution channels) to search for ways to meet their customers' requirements and improve the efficiency, timeliness, and cost of their operations. These initiatives spanned the entire chain of activities from the suppliers to the distribution of products to the end customers. Per the dictionary of the American Production and Inventory Control Society (APICS), the leading professional association for supply chain and operations management, the supply chain is defined as:

1. The processes from the initial raw materials to the ultimate consumption of the finished products linking across supplier-user companies; and

2. The functions within and outside a company that enable the value chain to make products and provide service to the customer

So, the supply chain is a superset of Porter's value chain concept that extends beyond the boundaries of the company both upstream and downstream, with a value chain(s) within the boundaries of the company's direct control.

EXHIBIT 7-6. **The Supply Chain Model**

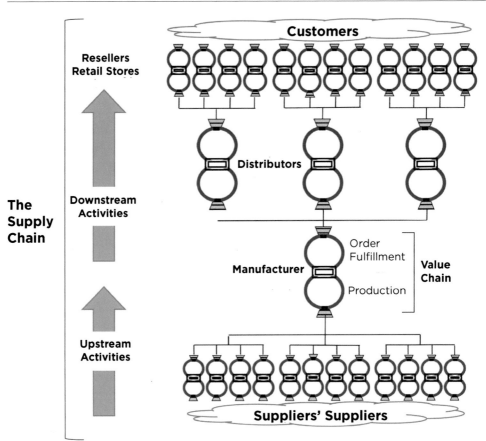

The complexity of the supply chain concept can be seen in Exhibit 7-7, where many companies, each with their own value chains, are linked in a spider web of business relationships that can reach from a few suppliers into hundreds of entities. In addition, each business in the supply chain has its own information system with computers, servers, networks, storage and security systems that are unique to that company. This represents a significant challenge to effective communication and the collaboration needed for an efficient supply chain network.

Supply Chain Management (SCM) emerged as a specific management discipline in the 1990s with a focus on satisfying the end users' requirements with products and services that depended on the performance of the suppliers.[9] Supply Chain Management grew as a business practice as information technology (Enterprise Resource Planning and other enterprise applications) evolved to improve communication and data sharing within the company as well as between the company and its suppliers. The timely communication of information regarding supplier orders, forecasts, shipping schedules, status, etc., is critical to the coordination of material flow to the production process. Prior to the emergence of the ubiquitous Internet, standards for supplier and transportation communication, such as the Electronic Data Interchange (EDI) were developed by the National Institute of Standards and Technology so that supply chain messages could be transmitted in a standard format that was independent of an individual company's computers and software. Today, the Internet and email have made communication easier and new standards continue to be developed to meet the needs of companies and suppliers working in a global network.

Supply Chain Management techniques became more sophisticated and widely adopted as leading business schools and management consulting firms conducted intriguing research on supply chain problems. Large corporations found excessive inventory positions and misaligned production in the supply chain due to multiple factors, including the lack of visibility (information sharing) of end user fluctuations in demand. These demand variations were amplified as they moved away from the end user purchasing at the retail level and caused what is called the "bullwhip effect," originally defined by Jay Wright Forrester with MIT's Sloan School of Management in his landmark book, *Industrial Dynamics*.[10] Forrester worked with General Electric, who sought to understand the dramatic fluctuations in production in their Kentucky appliance plant that necessitated the reduction of 50 percent of the workforce during certain years. He used innovative simulation techniques to identify the fluctuations in the network that were based on 1) limited visibility across the supply chain and 2) internal management policies for hiring.

As Forrester developed his theories and simulation models into *Systems Dynamics*, he was able to model complex distribution systems with hundreds of variables including management policies. He found that these simulation models could predict the behavior of the complex business operations and supply chain networks, but the managers, based on their own intuitive assumptions and personal perspectives, would make decisions that ultimately were counter-productive to the business.[11]

These findings were taught at MIT Sloan School of Management and many other business schools through the Beer Distribution Game. Teams of four MBA students, each acting as a company in the supply chain, would compete to run a beer distribution chain simulation over 60–90 minutes. Teams made decisions on production and distribution volumes utilizing the beer game simulation software and they nearly always ended up with excessive inventories and excessive costs for one or more participants.

Many corporations have implemented supply chain initiatives to improve communication, reduce costs, and promote just-in-time supplier sourcing to reduce production inventories to minimum levels. Software vendors and management consulting firms have provided new tools and consulting assistance to enable improved information flow regarding the price, availability, configuration, and status of purchased supplier parts, subassemblies, and services from the supplier network. The goal of these Supply Chain Management initiatives is to streamline the entire supply chain to improve production speed and quality, and ultimately deliver a high-quality product in a shorter timeframe to the end customer.

CHAPTER 8

Customer-Driven Competitive Strategies

8.1 Customer Perceived Value and Competitive Advantage

Business operation strategies are driven by the company's mission to deliver valuable goods and services produced with a competitive advantage. At the core of competitive advantage is the value that targeted customers place on the goods and services provided by the company. Value is defined by the customers in the chosen market segment(s) and the business's operation strategy that should be aligned with those value definitions.[1] The value of the goods and services as it is understood by the customer is called Customer Perceived Value (CPV). It is quite difficult to define this value since there are numerous benefit and cost attributes, and each customer has their own set of attributes that make up their perception of value. Exhibit 8.1 shows the basic equation of perceived value— benefit divided by cost—along with the *value attributes* for benefit and cost.

A key takeaway here is the critical interplay of the customer-driven value perspective and competitive advantage of the goods and services that a manufacturer provides. CPV can be influenced by powerful marketing efforts by product companies, but marketing only goes so far to influence customer perception. CPV changes as new trends emerge in the target market, and major fluctuations in CPV will result in product and operational changes that require corporate agility, new product innovation, willingness to change, and investment to maintain market position and brand significance. Competitive advantage is closely linked to the company's ability to understand the market's CPV, whether that is the latest

innovative functionality, lower cost, or greatest match to specific needs (customization). In the twenty-first century, companies can no longer sit on their
competitive strategy for long periods of time, since the market and business
environment is changing at an increasing rate.

EXHIBIT 8-1. **Customer Perceived Value**

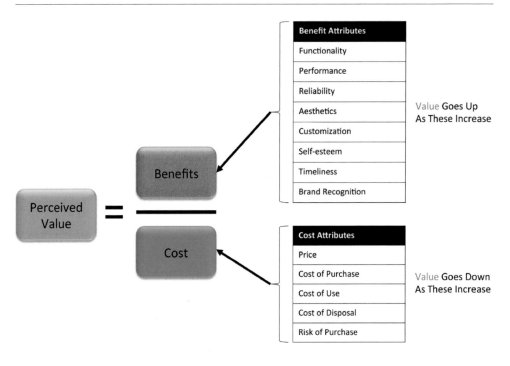

Key Principal: Competitive advantage is closely linked to the company's ability to
understand the market's CPV.

Here are a couple of interesting examples of the interaction of CPV and
competitive advantage.

8.2 **Example 1:**
Customer Perceived Value
in the Smartphone Industry

One example of how benefit and cost attributes define the value of a product and competitive advantage is evident when we consider purchasing a smartphone. Since smartphones are at the high end of the spectrum of available cell phones, the benefits of functionality, aesthetics, self-esteem, and brand name recognition will attract consumers willing to pay a premium price for their smartphone. For many users, especially the millennium generation purchasers, their phone is an integral part of their everyday lives with texting, social networking, applications, and phone calls dominating their activities. Having the latest phone with the best functionality and coolness factor drives their self-esteem as they show it off to their friends. Apple's iPhone has been a leading player in the on-going innovation of smartphones with almost limitless functionality due to the plethora of applications.

In August of 2005, Google bought the phone operating system developer, Android, Inc., signaling its intention to enter the smartphone software business.[2] The first commercially available Android smartphone was released in October of 2008 with the launch of the HTC Dream Phone and Android Market (now Google Play), the application store for Android.[3] The competitive battle for market share heated up dramatically as Google and Verizon together launched a $100M marketing campaign in late 2009, touting "Droid Does" with a sci-fi, robotic advertising blitz that targeted tech-savvy, early adopter young males in their twenties and thirties.[4] This campaign helped build Android's brand name and boldly stated that Droid had better functionality than Apple's iPhone.

Since their inception, smartphone functionality has been tied to the number of applications that run on the platform. In 2008, Steve Jobs announced that the iPhone had 500 available applications and indicated that this was one of the biggest announcements of his career, thus emphasizing the power of applications to drive the functionality, and competitive advantage, at the time.[5] Today, both Apple's iTunes Store and Google's Google Play *each* have more than 1.2 million applications available for smartphones and tablets.[6,7] The innovation race for more features in the smartphone itself and new applications has evolved with the typical "leap frog" advances by each competitor. Each competitor rolled out the latest features, and application counts grew at astonishing rates. However, because of the massive numbers of applications for each platform, the number of applications became "neutralized" as a functionality value attribute. Recently, the form factor (screen size, watch device) and battery life have become increasingly important as aesthetics and performance value attributes, indicating that product benefit attributes can change dramatically over time. Smartphone manufacturers continue to innovate to meet their customers' interests and needs, creating swings in competitive advantage related to product superiority.

8.3 Example 2: Customer Perceived Value in the Automotive Industry

A second example of how the benefit and cost attributes combine to create CPV is found when purchasing a car. In this case, the cost of the car is a dominant attribute for perceived value because the automobile and its related gas and maintenance expenses (aggregated as transportation) are the second largest category of personal expenditures in the U.S. behind housing.[8]

EXHIBIT 8-2. **Average U.S. Consumer Expenditures 2011–2013**

Item	2011	2012	2013	Percent change 2011-2012	Percent change 2012-2013
Average annual expenditures:					
Total......	$49,705	$51,442	$51,100	3.5	-0.7
Food......	6,458	6,599	6,602	2.2	0.0
At home......	3,838	3,921	3,977	2.2	1.4
Away from home......	2,620	2,678	2,625	2.2	-2.0
Housing......	16,803	16,887	17,148	0.5	1.5
Apparel and services......	1,740	1,736	1,604	-0.2	-7.6
Transportation......	8,293	8,998	9,004	8.5	0.1
Healthcare......	3,313	3,556	3,631	7.3	2.1
Entertainment......	2,572	2,605	2,482	1.3	-4.7
Cash contributions......	1,721	1,913	1,834	11.2	-4.1
Personal insurance and pensions......	5,424	5,591	5,528	3.1	-1.1
All other expenditures......	3,382	3,557	3,267	5.2	-8.2
Consumer unit characteristics:					
Number of consumer units (000's)......	122,287	124,416	125,670		
Average age of reference person......	49.7	50.0	50.1		
Average number in consumer unit:......					
People......	2.5	2.5	2.5		
Earners......	1.3	1.3	1.3		
Vehicles......	1.9	1.9	1.9		
Percent homeowner......	64.9	64.3	63.7		
Income before taxes......	$63,685	$65,596	$63,784	3.0	-2.8

A savvy automobile buyer looks at a wide spectrum of value attributes, including a consideration of the *lifetime costs* associated with the vehicle. Per Consumer Reports, the median "vehicle cost-to-own" is $9,100 per year for the first five years.[9] At $56,500 for total cost of ownership for five years, the CPV "cost-of-use" value attribute is typically more than the original cost of the vehicle. The breakdown of "cost-of-use" is shown in Exhibit 8-3 as owner costs.

EXHIBIT 8-3. **Total Cost of Ownership of Median Vehicles**

Comparing Owner Cost Percentages Across Different Point in Time

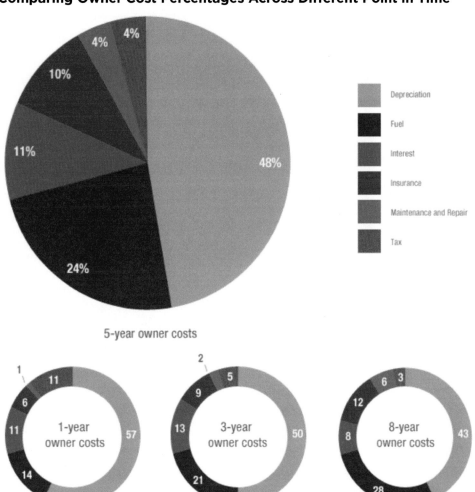

Each car purchaser has their own set of value attributes that they balance to determine the best value. Some buyers are on a budget and research the best price broken down to monthly loan or lease amounts and cost of ownership; those interested in speed and handling are into performance values (horsepower, torque, handling, towing capacity); while soccer Moms are into the child-oriented features and safety aspects of their mini-van wagon. With the huge U.S. market for new and used cars—17.5 million cars and light trucks sold in 2015[10]—automobile manufacturers and dealers have sorted the vehicles into classes and categories that meet the specific value attributes for each customer segment.

CPV and the related value equation can vary dramatically, especially when viewed over time. A customer's perception is different for each product category, industry, product/service mix, and economic situation, thereby presenting a significant challenge to the marketing department to stay in touch with the customer's changing value perspective. During times of economic strife, the value equation can swing dramatically toward the cost side of the value equation, as happened during the 1974 oil embargo when gas supply was dramatically reduced and prices soared.

At the time, GM, Ford, and Chrysler were selling 8–11 million cars a year with the greatest profit found in the largest, heaviest vehicles. The financial-oriented thinking at the time was that gas was cheap and it was more profitable to make larger, less efficient vehicles. Customers had been going along with the bigger-is-better philosophy until the 1974 oil embargo. They were shocked when gas prices rose and availability became a major issue, with long lines at the gas station. Car purchasers changed their buying habits and began looking for smaller, lighter weight vehicles with better gas mileage. The typical U.S. car got 13 miles per gallon, while the "econo-box" cars from Nissan, Honda, Toyota, and Volkswagen were getting more than twice that mileage. These inexpensive vehicles with better miles-per-gallon gas consumption swept into the global car markets and captured a significant market share from established U. S. car manufacturers offering only large, gas guzzling vehicles at the time.[11] The result was a significant shift in competitive advantage and market share over the next few years as U.S. car makers struggled to produce the low-end, gas-efficient automobiles that the market desired. So, it can be seen that CPV is an integral driver for the business's competitive strategy and related operations structures.

8.4 **Advances in Competitive Strategy Theories**

There have been several relevant advances in business theory that address the strategies that, when pursued diligently over time, produce a competitive advantage and profitability for the company. Competitive advantage is directly linked to an in-depth understanding of the target market and the buyer's perception of value (Customer Perceived Value). Only when the CPV is clearly understood and the value activities of the value chain optimized to deliver the targeted value, will competitive advantage emerge in a measurable way.

In his 1980 book, *Competitive Strategy*, Michael Porter pointed out that a company can realize above-average performance in the long run with a sustainable competitive advantage.[12] He stated that there are two basic types of competitive advantage—cost advantage and differentiation—that when combined with a third factor—scope of activities—produce three generic competitive advantage strategies as described in Exhibit 8-4.

EXHIBIT 8-4. **Michael Porter's Generic Strategies**

	Broad	
Competitive Scope	1. Cost Leadership	2. Differentiation
	3a. Cost Focus	3b. Differentiation Focus
Narrow (Niche)		

The long-term performance advantage in this approach is based on the company's ability to produce its goods and services with one competitive advantage (cost or differentiation) while remaining at parity with competitors in the other advantage category. In addition, he states that a company must choose to compete on a broad market scope or a narrow market scope (niche) to be successful. The niche strategy of focusing on a narrow market is to identify and pursue a market segment that has different needs from the broader market. The long-term success of this niche strategy depends on the ability of the company to maintain its competitive advantage as other niche competitors or broad market companies attempt to match the established cost or differentiation advantage. Success in any of the general strategies is dependent on the ability of the company to become the cost or differentiation leader, distancing itself from industry rivals versus striving to be the leader, but remaining stuck in the middle of several rivals.

In January 1992 Michael Treacy and Fred Wiersema published an article in the *Harvard Business Review* that presented an expanded view of competitive advantage based on *value disciplines*.[13] Starting from the customer perspective, they found that successful companies pursued one of three competitive strategies aligned to customer value—*operational excellence, customer intimacy,* and *product leadership*. As presented in their article, long-term performance requires a company to excel in one value discipline and remain competent in the other two disciplines.

Key Principal: A competitive strategy is formed by excelling in one value discipline and remaining competent in the other two.

In Exhibit 8-5, the three value disciplines are presented with a summary of the overall strategy and tactics to achieve each value discipline.

EXHIBIT 8-5. **Three Value Disciplines**

Value Discipline	Strategy	Tactics
Operational Excellence	Lead the industry in price and convenience	• minimize overhead costs • reduce process steps and waste • optimize process across departments, channels, and supply chain • enhance IT systems to measure demand, cycle time, and productivity
Customer Intimacy	Continually customize products and services to meet customerspecific needs to attain customer loyalty	• understand individual customer requirements in detail • focus on customer lifetime value • segment marketing and production of goods and services • enhance IT systems to understand buying trends, features, and customer profiles • invest in education of employees related to customer needs/solutions
Product Leadership	Continuously develop new products and services to lead the market in innovation	• identify customer problems and make new solutions • enable a creative development environment • take products to market quickly • avoid bureaucracy to be flexible • enhance IT systems to support development and risk management

In essence, Treacy and Wiersema provided a cost leadership and two differentiation strategies per Porter's competitive advantage model. For any case of competitive advantage, the key is understanding the customer perceived value of the buyer and optimize the business value chain to deliver a valuable product or service that matches the buyer's needs.

CHAPTER 9

Selecting a Competitive Strategy

A SUSTAINABLE COMPETITIVE ADVANTAGE requires a detailed analysis of the target market and an objective evaluation of the company's capabilities to deliver value to buyers. Getting direct, honest feedback from existing customers is essential, especially if there are subtle requirements that customers are reluctant to mention. Once a competitive strategy is selected, there is a need to stay focused on the strategy and continue investment over a length of time. Measurement of success and nudging of the tiller to keep the ship on course should occur based on a long-term horizon. As found through in-depth research in Jim Collins' book, *Good to Great,* it is wise to focus over time on a single strategy with meaningful performance metrics.[1] This is called the *Hedgehog Concept*. Rather than wander from strategy to strategy too quickly, the management team makes only slight directional changes over several years to achieve a competitive advantage. A key metric is associated with the Hedgehog strategy to drive optimization, investment, and compensation over time. In *Good to Great*, the example presented is Walmart's focus on *dollars per store visit* as the key metric that drives their Operational Excellence strategy (low cost and convenience).

9.1 Profiling the Buyer

The first step is to identify the key decision maker/buyer in the target market. This may seem straightforward, but it involves thoughtful research to determine who the key decision maker is in a large organization, as opposed to recommenders and influencers. Purchasing managers, for example, may be the primary point of communication for the purchasing decision, but a director in the business unit ultimately makes the purchasing decision in the approval chain. In consumer markets, identifying the customer profile in a target market involves research into a variety of factors—age range, geographic location, gender, income range, ethnic characteristics, and other factors.

Once the buyer has been identified and profiled, then the customer perceived value (CPV) analysis is conducted to understand how the buyer sees value and makes the decision to move from interest to purchase in the sales funnel. The value of this information cannot be underestimated because it drives all other aspects of competitive strategy.

Key Principal: A competitive strategy is customer-centric and driven by market-pull, as opposed to creating goods and services and pushing them to the market.

Gaining insight into the buyer's perceived value can be obtained by one-on-one key client conversations, carefully constructed focus groups with an open-minded perspective, or by hiring customer personnel to bring their many years of knowledge and experience inside the company. Identifying and prioritizing the full spectrum of *buyer characteristics,* as well as the *purchasing process,* is needed to complete the customer perceived value analysis.

Although it is important to understand the nuances of the buyer's perceived value perspective, analyzing the cost factors versus benefit factors should be the first step (see Exhibit 8-1). If the buyer is primarily driven by cost and convenience, then this indicates following a low-cost competitive strategy, *operational excellence.* If the buyer values a highly custom product or service to meet their specific needs, then a *customer intimacy* strategy is indicated. If the buyer desires innovative products that provide new levels of benefit, then a *product leadership* strategy should be pursued.

9.2 Analyzing the Value Activities in the Company

Once the customer profile is complete, the company conducts a self-analysis of its primary value chain. There typically are more than one value chain in the company delivering key elements that are valued by the buyer, but at this point only the primary business value chain is considered, as it drives most of the business income. Each value chain element from sales and marketing to procurement is evaluated and scored as high (4-5), medium (3), or low (1-2), where high is excelling, medium is average, and low needs improvement. This quick analysis helps identify strengths and weaknesses relative to a rational decision on which competitive strategy to follow.

A key benefit of the strengths and weaknesses mapping exercise is to develop a more in-depth understanding of the key value-generating components of the company and how they depend on each other to operate efficiently. In Chapter 10 each competitive strategy is linked to areas of the Dynamic Value Chain that need to perform to a high degree to drive sustainable advantage. Comparing the current strengths and weaknesses of the value chain elements to the areas of optimization provides a rough gap analysis for investment planning. To better understand the current costs of each area, a cost-based analysis (Activity-Based Costing study) can be conducted to allocate costs to the major elements of the value chain. Later, these costs could be used to estimate the costs of optimizing the value chain to meet the competitive strategy.

9.3 Selecting the Competitive Strategy

The approach suggested in this book is to combine Porter's generic strategies with those of Treacy and Wiersema. First the decision is made to be a niche or broad player in the market. A niche strategy requires extensive knowledge and capabilities in the niche market, whereas a broad strategy requires extensive supply chain and distribution channels. If a business is a start-up or new, it usually makes sense to focus on a niche until profits are sustainable.

The next step is for the management team to pick one of the three value disciplines to pursue in line with external customer perceived value and internal value-producing capabilities. Here are the core strategies and suggested value activity areas that, when improved, can result in a competitive advantage.

EXHIBIT 9-1. **Competitive Strategy**

As stated by Treacy and Wiersema, to achieve competitive advantage, a company must excel in the selected value discipline and be at least competent in the other value disciplines. The mapping exercise of value chain elements gives insights into the areas of excellence and areas for improvement to focus investments that align with the selected competitive strategy.

Key Principal: For long-term success, a firm must excel at the chosen competitive strategy and be at least competent in other areas.

CHAPTER 10

Optimizing the Business for Competitive Advantage

THIS CHAPTER PRESENTS THE KEY CHARACTERISTICS of the three value disciplines, illustrates the value chain elements that must be strengthened for superiority, and provides case studies illustrating the business decisions and optimization to achieve a winning competitive strategy.

10.1 Operational Excellence Strategy

Here low-cost goods and services, convenience, and efficient processes are top areas for optimization. Business investment is focused on reducing business cost through identification and elimination of waste, process innovation, and creative delivery channels to make goods and services less expensive and easily available. Greater operational efficiency reduces internal costs of production and distribution, which allows the company to lower prices. Procurement and supply chain partners must keep up with the highly efficient business operations to keep production on schedule. Finally, mass marketing communication is required to build awareness of customer savings. If successful, the volume of sales is significant, which builds the profits and cash flow of the company.

EXHIBIT 10-1. **Areas of Optimization for Operational Excellence Strategy**

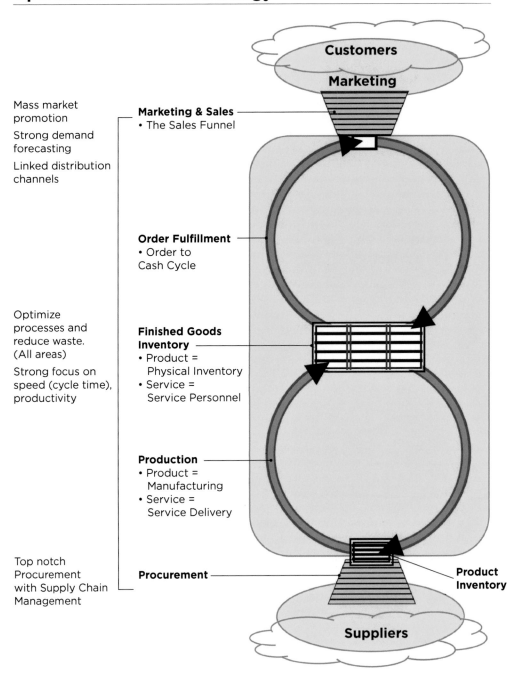

Operational Excellence Case—Sweet Goods Bakery

A good friend of mine is the president of Sweet Goods Bakery (SGB), which has focused on an operational excellence strategy for many years resulting in outstanding business results. SGB was founded in 1934 and manufactures sweet snacks including donuts, apple fritters, cinnamon rolls, fried pies, and pecan and coconut pies. It also provides fresh/frozen pie tart shells and fruit/custard fillings, as well as pie dough sheets for baking pies, cobblers, and meat pies. In addition, the company offers private label manufacturing and co-packaging services. It serves vendor suppliers, private label customers, retail and convenience stores, and industrial food clients.

The current president took over the family-owned business from his father after completing a top- notch education that included Harvard Business School. His father stayed on to transition the business management over a period of years. One of the early improvements that they made involved changes to the chemistry of their dough that improves the quality and extends the shelf life of the finished baked products. This product innovation has continued to provide a competitive advantage for several decades, as their customers value the higher quality and extended shelf life. After the initial improvements from product innovation, the president began a crusade to improve multiple aspects of the operation to reduce costs and eliminate waste.

Most of SGB business is derived from delivery of finished bakery goods to large industrial food clients through daily orders with a one- to five-day turnaround. There are no long-term sales contracts with these customers, even though the top customers treat SGB as an integral production plant. To reduce the risk associated with the lack of long-term contracts, a strong customer service approach is utilized in the sales and marketing area to provide daily communication and order status. In addition, the largest buyers have provided access to their purchasing information systems, so SGB can access and update orders on-line. The resulting integrated supply chain capability provides increased convenience for the large buyers to check on order status without a delay. The customer service approach has evolved over the years to the point where SGB has become a trusted advisor— the buyers now ask SGB for advice on a regular basis.

In pursuit of the operational excellence strategy, the president has consistently focused on reducing cost and improving operation efficiency across the company.

He is passionate about reducing waste and improving operations to gain incremental advantages over time. On the supply chain side, he negotiates every contract with suppliers to seek ways to reduce his raw material costs and improve delivery schedules to minimize raw material inventory levels. In product delivery, he made significant transportation cost savings by thinking out of the box. SGB worked with their shipping company to redesign the cargo area of their trucks to allow for double stacking the pallet loads of finished goods.

A general manager oversees the daily operations and is motivated to achieve the short-term order completion on time to meet buyer requirements. The general manager and the president monitor order reports and production capacity daily to fine tune operations to meet demand. Identifying areas of operational waste and cost reduction falls back to the president, who reviews overtime reports and tracks ongoing operational issues looking for patterns that indicate an area for improvement. The potential operational enhancements are prioritized and the level of effort is roughly estimated to determine if the change can be integrated into the production schedule and if it is worth the effort.

Beyond the daily operational management regimen, the president and his sales team have regular communication with the buyers regarding new product introductions, end of life schedules, and purchasing forecasts. SGB is under constant pricing pressure from its buyers who are actively shopping the orders to multiple competitors. The president negotiates pricing using his quality and shelf-life advantage, reliable production schedule, and strong customer service approach to substantiate his pricing levels.

On an annual basis, SGB holds a sales meeting to review forecasts from its sales team. These forecasts have a limited horizon due to the short-term ordering of SGB customers. Long-term projects are initiated based on consistent production issues or introduction of new product lines (if there is solid business for the new product). Due to the lack of longer contracts, investments in a new production line or a new plant to meet potential market demand are considered very carefully before proceeding. When a major industrial customer filed for bankruptcy, SGB was faced with the potential of being out of business in six months, or doubling or tripling their business. After research and discussions with his customers, the president decided to invest in a new production line, which helped to double his revenues once the new line was operational.

Because of the constant attention and action related to an operational excellence strategy as a cost-focused provider with operational efficiency and convenience, SGB has realized a significant business outcome. The annual EBIT earnings for SGB have been higher than the industry average for many years. This exceptional result could only have been achieved with the passionate drive of the president to be engaged in every aspect of the business and use creative approaches to optimize his business toward the competitive advantage associated with the operational excellence strategy (his Hedgehog Concept).

Along the way, SGB has also engaged in product leadership (innovation) and customer intimacy activities to maintain a competency level in those areas. Interestingly, one of the current deliberations by the president relates to a new round of product innovation to create a healthy snack offering to drive future business. This highlights the need to excel in one value discipline while maintaining competency in the other two disciplines and shifting emphasis to respond to changing market or customer situations.

10.2 Product Leadership Strategy

Here product/service development (production cycle) is a key area for investment and optimization to produce new offerings on a regular basis. This frequently involves leapfrogging competitors in an emerging industry, creating a race to provide innovative solutions to customer needs (sometimes before the need is realized, ala Steve Jobs at Apple). Innovative products don't necessarily appeal to everyone in the market, but customers who seek out innovations purchase the new products, frequently paying a premium for the latest technology. Then, based on the word-of-mouth references from the innovators, product sales increase as early adopters begin to buy and expand sales volume.

If the product is a success, late adopters begin to buy as prices begin to decrease and the product has been validated by a couple of solid updates. Ultimately, this drives growth of product sales until the next round of innovation comes to market. For some industries, this innovation cycle may last for years, and for others, such as the fashion or cell phone industries, it can be an annual event with high expectations from industry analysts.

EXHIBIT 10-2. **Areas of Optimization for Product Leadership Strategy**

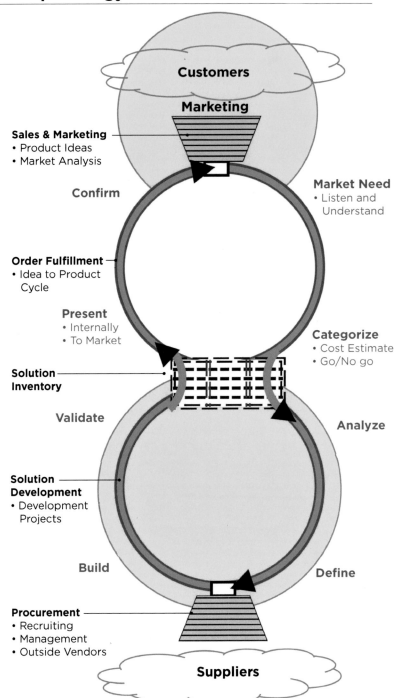

Strong customer interaction

Identify new product ideas

Communicate CPV and specifications accurately

Excellent decision making process with a view to team capacity

Invest in people with knowledge

Optimize the environment

Support creativity within limits

Deliver regular innovations

Customers

Marketing

Sales & Marketing
• Product Ideas
• Market Analysis

Confirm

Market Need
• Listen and Understand

Order Fulfillment
• Idea to Product Cycle

Present
• Internally
• To Market

Categorize
• Cost Estimate
• Go/No go

Solution Inventory

Validate

Analyze

Solution Development
• Development Projects

Build

Define

Procurement
• Recruiting
• Management
• Outside Vendors

Suppliers

Product leadership companies must excel at understanding the customer and CPV to seek out new innovations. The sales and marketing organization identifies new products or features from customer focus groups or one-on-one sales activities and communicates the customer requirements with great accuracy to the development group. The research and development group is encouraged to be creative, while managers work to deliver timely releases of new innovations. Finally, there is a strong focus on the hiring of and caring for talented people to drive innovation on a long-term basis.

Product Leadership Case—3M Corporation

Some notable industry leaders such as Corning, Apple, Microsoft, and 3M Corporation have adopted a product leadership strategy with a strategic focus and strong executive leadership to consistently pursue business optimization to create a competitive advantage. 3M Corporation (3M) the developer of Masking Tape, Scotch™ tape, Sticky Notes (Post-it®), and thousands of other products in the industrial, safety and graphics, electronics and energy, health care, and consumer markets, has long held a top-down driven product leadership strategy that has led to significant growth and profitability over decades. In 2015, 3M's operating income was $6.9B (23 percent) on total sales of $30.2B, while the innovation-focused research and development spending was $1.8B (5.8 percent of sales). Their decades-long relentless focus on innovation has progressed to the point that they release more than twenty new products a week, while delivering significant shareholder dividends of $4.10 per share in 2015.[1]

Continuing to excel at product leadership over an extended period, as 3M has done, requires a culture of innovation and extensive investment. Innovation must be considered as more than incremental improvements on the next release of the product. In 2002, 3M produced a fascinating book on its 100-year anniversary, *A Century of Innovation—The 3M Story*[2], that reviewed its history and corporate philosophy resulting in the outstanding financial outcomes listed above. The areas of optimization for the product leadership value chain in Exhibit 10-2 are listed along with the 3M evolutionary steps throughout their history.

Strong customer interaction: Time Tested Truths— "Ask your customers what quality is, then never let the standard slip."

Identify new product ideas: "A Tolerance for Tinkerers"—In 1920, 3M was focused on sandpaper products, but in 1923, Dick Drew spoke with an automotive body shop about a problem they had while painting cars. Existing tape would ruin the paint when pulled off after painting. In 1925, after two years of his own research, he invented Scotch masking tape. Later in 1937, based on Drew's sponsorship, the Central Research Laboratory was launched for new product research.

Analyze Customer Perceived Value: "Look Behind the Smokestacks"— William McKnight, 3M's 24-year-old sales manager in 1911, went to 29 customer locations and visited with the men on the production line to learn how 3M's products were used. He found that the products were disliked, so McKnight requested to be put in charge of 3M's production and quality control. He drove changes that improved quality, and never stopped going to their users for feedback.

Excellent decision-making process: By 1948, McKnight was president when he restructured 3M by creating divisions—individual profit centers that had the power, autonomy, and resources to run independently. Each division was small and remained close to the customers. If they grew too big, that's when McKnight's "divide and grow" philosophy took over—new businesses were spun off with new management teams resulting in new growth.

Invest in people with knowledge: Time Tested Truths— "Give good people opportunities, support them and watch them thrive."

Optimize the environment: In 1982, 3M had expanded into a market led by its Occupational Health and Environmental Safety Division (OH&ESD) with respirators and face masks, but their innovation pace was too slow. Bob Hershock changed the organization to a whole new approach called "cross-functional action teams." From 1986 to 1996, OH&ESD introduced 20 new products, and 10 out of the 11 products developed by the division's action teams—products with the highest potential—made it to market on time. Overall, the time involved in new product development was cut in half.

Support creativity within limits: Time Tested Truths— "A 'loose-tight' philosophy of management balances entrepreneurial action and corporate consistency where it matters most."

Deliver regular innovations: 3M used a key metric to track regular innovation—the percent of sales coming from products developed in the previous five years.

10.3 Customer Intimacy Strategy

This differentiation strategy focuses on knowing the customers and their intricate needs better than the competition. This strategy follows the "engineer to order" value chain, where each product or service is custom-built based on customer needs. These customers value the specialized solution to their specific needs and, consequently, will pay a premium for them. Investment to optimize the business with this value chain strategy is targeted at developing strong relationships leading to loyalty (and profitability) over time. Customer Intimacy value chains produce products or services that are one-off solutions for specific customers and their exacting specifications.

Professional service firms typically follow a customer intimacy strategy. For example, a leading architectural firm pursues a customer intimacy strategy to deliver custom designs that meet the specific needs of commercial clients. They must also remain competent in operational excellence (cost competitive and responsive), as well as competent in product leadership (innovation) by utilizing current building materials and techniques. For the firm to establish an advantage over their competitors, the partner/owners (sales and marketing function) must establish and maintain deep relationships with clients, and precisely understand and define the customer's requirements for the design of the building. Those requirements must then be effectively communicated throughout the design process (production) with quality reviews, so that the final commercial building design meets the customer's desired vision or budget. The ability of the firm to efficiently handle requirement changes throughout the design project must also be excellent to avoid mistakes and customer frustration (operational excellence).

EXHIBIT 10-3. **Areas of Optimization for Customer Intimacy Strategy**

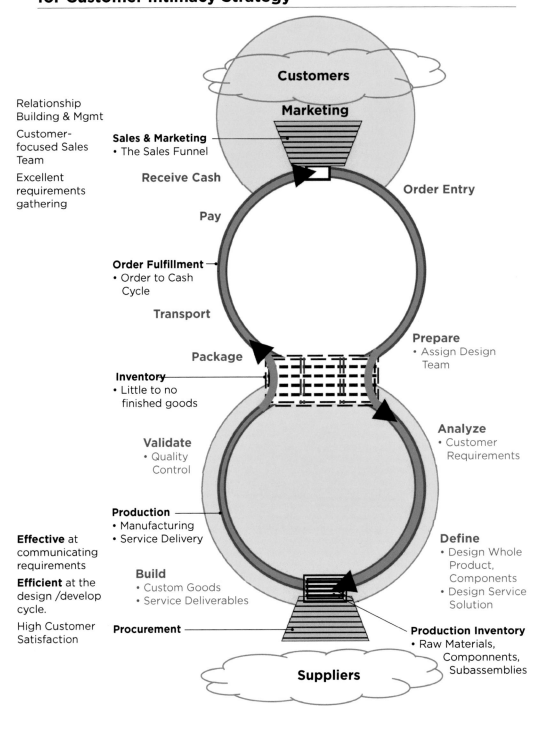

Relationship Building & Mgmt

Customer-focused Sales Team

Excellent requirements gathering

Customers

Marketing

Sales & Marketing
• The Sales Funnel

Receive Cash

Order Entry

Pay

Order Fulfillment
• Order to Cash Cycle

Transport

Prepare
• Assign Design Team

Package

Inventory
• Little to no finished goods

Analyze
• Customer Requirements

Validate
• Quality Control

Production
• Manufacturing
• Service Delivery

Effective at communicating requirements

Efficient at the design /develop cycle.

Define
• Design Whole Product, Components
• Design Service Solution

Build
• Custom Goods
• Service Deliverables

High Customer Satisfaction

Procurement

Production Inventory
• Raw Materials, Components, Subassemblies

Suppliers

A competitive advantage requires a consistent focus from the management team and long-term efforts to continuously develop and enhance the primary strategy, while maintaining competence in the other two value disciplines.

Customer Intimacy Case—Technology Reseller Company

A leading regional technology reseller company (TRC) had been successful in growing its business in the1990s and early 2000s, based on sales of Unix servers from Sun Microsystems, a major computer equipment manufacturer. TRC's business included a mix of product sales, implementation services for installation of the purchased equipment, and maintenance service contracts that provided the customer with technology support and upgrades to the operating system. TRC was following an operational excellence business model to provide low-cost quotes in competition with several other resellers, and then deliver the products quickly and conveniently to the customer. The factors of low cost, operational efficiency and convenience were driven by the commoditization of hardware equipment and the demanding, fast-paced purchasing requirements of their Information Technology (IT) customers. A bid process was frequently involved, and typically the low-cost bid won the deal. The customer's IT department would then apply pressure to get the equipment installed and running on a short, unrealistic schedule. This forced TRC to optimize their business toward fast quoting processes, extensive discounting to win the business, and a service implementation team that was available to install the equipment on short notice. This last factor resulted in lower consultant utilization due to high bench time waiting for the next deal to close to begin the installation project.

On January 28, 2010, Oracle Corporation, the world's leading database and ERP software provider, acquired Sun Microsystems for $7.4B, in line with an industry-wide consolidation trend. This acquisition positioned Oracle as a major technology vendor in competition with HP, IBM, Dell, and Cisco, that had been acquiring software companies to expand their reach beyond hardware.

Shortly after the acquisition, the parent company made several disruptive changes to the reseller channel agreements that affected the resellers' ability to sell the expensive computer equipment and to receive annual payments from maintenance agreements. These changes represented a major threat to TRC's successful business, requiring a significant retooling of the business model to avoid a serious decline in their revenues.

TRC's president made several immediate changes and then reset the sales objectives to transition the business model from operational excellence to customer intimacy. The president knew that the key to this transition would be a rapid shift in sales focus and operations toward value-added consulting services over product sales and related installation services.

Reduce Product Sales Focus—Within two weeks of Oracle's announcement, TRC made changes to the product sales support team. The account managers went back to generating their own quotes. In addition, the sales team was directed to pursue consulting service deals with some product drag versus a large product-only sales opportunity with lower gross profit margin and more competition. The consulting resources were strong in security and networking, so the marketing and sales activities were concentrated in those areas. The sales team began to seek out customers who had the need for their technical strengths rather than chasing any customer with a product deal.

Improve Consultant Utilization—Prior to 2010, the consultant utilization factor (percent billable time) was not a significant metric since product sales revenue and gross profit were the major focal points, and consultants were frequently involved in the product selling process. Fortunately, TRC had established a beachhead by hiring and retaining top-notch consultants over time. TRC customers recognized the quality level of the consultants, which became a key selling point for the lead-with-services approach. The president modified the compensation structure by establishing a utilization target of 65 percent billable time for all consultants, and then provided a bonus for the consultants if their utilization exceeded the target. This compensation technique, in combination with the consultant's ability to identify opportunities within the account, has worked extremely well with several consultants exceeding 100 percent utilization in 2013. The utilization range across all the consultants is now 80–109 percent, a dramatic improvement over the 50 percent utilization prior to 2010.

Invest in Consultant Education—Since the quality of the consultant is based extensively in their technical knowledge, TRC has invested in technical education to keep them on the leading edge of technology. Customers believe (perceived quality) that the consultants know the technology and have worked with numerous client situations to deliver an optimized service engagement (value). Not only is the investment in education related to the cost of the training, but the time allowed for training must be considered as well. Setting the consultant utilization target too high results in reluctance by service managers to allow time for training. This is a striking element in the shift from operational excellence, where getting to the next billable job is all consuming, to customer intimacy, where the knowledge of the consultant and his ability to understand the customer's environment are tantamount. In this case, TRC included training time along with the billable time in the utilization target.

Innovative New Services—Another step that TRC took to move to customer intimacy was to create an annual contract service that provided a pooled resource service for the customer. In addition to the ad hoc consultant service with a non-discounted rate and custom projects with statement of work contacts, the new service provides the client with access to a range of consultants specialized in various technology domains. This creative approach is very attractive to customers because the resource pool provides a broad set of technical knowledge from multiple consultants for the price of one. The customer has the flexibility to choose the consultant they need at the time for specific work efforts. TRC gets the strategic advantage of having their consultants residing inside the customer environment, additionally providing optics into customer situations that could lead to follow-on business to TRC. Greater understanding of the customer environment and situation is the cornerstone of customer intimacy, where custom solutions are defined that meet the customer's specific needs.

Management Reporting—Making a major transition in a company's business model requires management reporting that provides insights into key optimization metrics.

- **Short-term reporting:** Monthly product and consulting gross profit by account manager provides a productivity measurement of the sales team. As the deals are bid, proposed gross profit is closely monitored, with any deal below the 10 percent level requiring management approval. The focus on gross profit is a shift from the top line revenue metric of the product-centric reporting prior to 2010. Company revenues and gross profit are tracked carefully, and any significant changes in the trend line trigger a drill-down into the reasons why there was a change. In addition, TRC watches billable hours (utilization) monthly for each engineer with two metrics—gross utilization and net utilization that factors in training time, so as not to penalize the consultant's bonus when they are in training. TRC's president indicated that it is important to make tough decisions and take corrective action if a consultant's utilization trend was not meeting targets.

- **Mid-term reporting:** Marketing programs are planned, executed, and tracked on a quarterly basis. Frequently these marketing activities target new technologies or upgrades that are attractive to their specific customers. Knowing what the customers have in their IT environments and when they might need to refresh their equipment is important to the customer intimacy marketing. Evaluation of results after each quarter is done on a sales opportunity generation basis rather than a program cost basis, which maintains a positive focus and encourages experimentation.

- **Long-term reporting:** A top customer report provides revenue and gross profit information for each major account. Noticeable year-over-year variations are researched and the reasons documented. The detailed knowledge of customer situations has increased dramatically as the customer intimacy business model has been implemented. After annual business reports are generated, a budgeting process is initiated to establish the financial targets and operational metrics for the coming year.

Business Results of Transitioning to Customer Intimacy Model—
Today, the sales team is still chasing deals opportunistically, but there is
more focus on leading with services and long-term customer relationships.
While consultants are on-site, they are educating the client on new technology
features and benefits, which is leading to product sales and more services.
Overall, the volatile nature of pure product reselling—where revenue spikes
occur when a big deal closes—has been replaced by a more consistent and
predictable revenue stream.

Although TRC's product revenue has declined by 50 percent from 2009 to
2013, their consulting revenue has increased 160 percent and the consulting
gross profit has increased 269 percent over the four years. Ultimately, the transition from an operational excellence to customer intimacy business model is still
evolving, but TRC has successfully completed a major business restructuring
that avoided a potentially devastating outcome for the company.

10.4 Shifting Competitive Strategies Over Time

Before we leave this chapter, a note about shifting competitive strategies over
time. As industries grow and evolve, there are shifts in customer perceived value
that can destroy a competitive advantage of existing companies. A classic example
is evident in the early automotive industry of the late 1800s and early 1900s.
Early automobiles were custom built by coach builders for wealthy customers
who wanted the latest innovation. They competed on a product leadership strategy
to continue to develop new features and models for customers who desired the
latest innovation of performance and luxury. The popularity of automobiles was
growing in the early 1900s and a mass market was on the horizon, when a young
entrepreneur named Henry Ford envisioned a "car for the common man." With
incredible drive and determination, he began producing low-cost automobiles
that more people could afford, with standard features and a production facility
that became increasingly operationally efficient. In this case, a product leadership

strategy was replaced by an operational excellence strategy that could reach a broader market of customers who valued a lower price. This is typical of industries that experience huge growth as market demand increases and products are commoditized.

CHAPTER 11

Macro Performance Indicators of the Business Value Chain

11.1 Macro Performance Indicators, the Keys to Business Optimization

Tracking the performance of the business value chain and competitive strategy progress requires a few Macro Performance Indicators (MPIs) that provide high-level business insights as opposed to thousands of departmental Key Performance Indicators (KPIs) that have grown over years of performance management and management by objectives. Providing the clarity of these MPIs gives executives and managers a set of "big dial" performance metrics that help *align individual departmental contributions across the enterprise*. As initiatives are envisioned and executed to improve a MPI, multiple departments are required to work together to generate results. This creates natural alignment of purpose within the company.

Key Principal: Macro Performance Indicators provide the "big dial" metrics that promote multi-departmental alignment and leads to significant company performance if pursued over time.

Before we jump into defining MPIs, let's review a point about financial reports. The income statements, cash flow statements, and balance sheets produced from accounting and finance are still core scoreboard documents at the overall business or business unit level. These reports provide easily understood guidance on the overall financial status and performance utilizing standardized rules of accounting data allocation. MPIs on the other hand, provide insights into the key underlying elements of the business capabilities that must combine effectively to drive the performance at the financial level. Focusing attention on these MPIs allows multiple departments to coordinate their efforts to have measurable impacts on performance in a big way, and ultimately impact the bottom line of the business as shown in the financial reports.

The following MPIs, by value discipline strategy, are presented for consideration, discussion, and future research. Readers are encouraged to evaluate and apply those that seem to be most applicable to their business.

11.2 Macro Performance Indicators for Operational Excellence

As seen in Exhibit 8-5, the operational excellence value discipline strives to *lead the industry in price and convenience*. In many cases, operational excellence is associated with a broad market strategy because there are commodity goods and services involved. For a company to build a competitive advantage in a commodity market, it must excel at operations so that it can keep prices lower, and the company must seek out ways to provide its goods and services as conveniently as possible.

Operational Excellence MPI#1—Muda Waste Reduction

The concept of Lean Management emerged in the late 1980s from concepts developed at Toyota—Toyota Production System, but it has its roots in Henry Ford's work in industrial engineering and process improvement in the early 1900s.[1] The goal is to reduce waste so that an efficient operation can be achieved. In the Dynamic Value Chain concept, this would apply to both the order fulfillment and production cycles.

Muda is the primary waste of an operation that leads to delays, rework, and poor quality. Muda waste can be broken down into the following categories:

- Transport (moving products that are not actually required to perform the processing)

- Inventory (all components, work in process, and finished product not being processed)

- Motion (people or equipment moving or walking more than is required to perform the processing)
- Waiting (waiting for the next production step, interruptions of production during shift change)
- Overproduction (production ahead of demand)
- Over Processing (resulting from poor tool or product design creating activity)
- Defects (the effort involved in inspecting for and fixing defects)[1]

Lean manufacturing metrics and techniques have grown extensively throughout the 1990s to today. The Macro Performance Indicator, Muda, is used to measure levels of operational waste so managers can act to reduce it through process optimization and just-in-time supply techniques. A good definition of the actual Muda MPI (as well as Muri and Mura) calculations can be found in an article in the *International Journal of Lean Thinking*, titled "Waste Management Techniques for Lean Companies."[2]

Operational Excellence MPI#2—Cycle Time MPIs

Customers who value low-cost goods and services want fast, convenient delivery. There are numerous advances in business models based on these factors, such as Uber. The founders of Uber came up with their business idea when they were in Paris and couldn't find a taxi late at night. The Uber application later would allow a user to book a ride from their iPhone, watch the driver approach on a digital street map, and pay for the ride on-line—resulting in a much more convenient and fast service.

The Macro Performance Indicator for cycle time is applied to both cycles in the value chain—order fulfillment and production. Order fulfillment cycle time starts when the order is received and ends when cash has been received. McDonalds, for example, has honed their order fulfillment cycle time (MPI) to the point that McDonalds' drive-through service receives cash in about two minutes from the beginning of the order fulfillment cycle.

The production cycle time (MPI) starts when the order has been entered into the information technology system (order entry), until the finished goods or services have been placed into inventory for packaging and shipment to the customer. Building a Ferrari as a custom order for a sports car enthusiast, for example, involves a production cycle that starts after the customer order has been entered into Ferrari's order entry application. The car is built at the Maranello factory in Italy to the specific requirements of the customer, and then shipped to the car dealer in the U.S. This production cycle can be frustratingly lengthy for the enthusiast who is dreaming of his new car. If the production cycle time is too long, the buyer may cancel his order and take his business elsewhere.

The challenge of operational excellence is to complete the cycles in acceptable time periods per customer expectations. The cycle time MPIs may get shorter and shorter as customer expectations are reset by competitors that succeed in speeding up their operations.

Operational Excellence MPI#3—Average Order Value (AOV)

Big box retailers, like Walmart, pursue an operational excellence strategy with a broad focus (rather than a niche focus) with mass marketing of low prices and a continuous drive to optimize their operations to reduce internal costs. Walmart has diversified the available goods on their stores' shelves to provide convenient, one-stop shopping for busy shoppers. As a result, their Average Order Value (AOV) has risen over time. AOV is simply the value of all sales for a period divided by the number of transactions. Many companies use revenue per order, which can apply to goods sold in retail stores as well as service orders (contracts). Given the previous interest in using gross profit as an indicator of value, it is recommended that AOV be calculated by taking the gross profit divided by the number of orders.

Operational Excellence MPI#4—Supply Chain Volume Statistics MPI

Large-scale business operations with extensive supply-side sourcing and sell-side distribution need to have an information system that provides awareness of flow rates at critical points, from raw materials and assemblies produced by suppliers, through the firm's production cycle, to the final distribution through warehouses to retailers or consumers. In the article, "Supply Chain 2025: Planning Today for Tomorrow,"[3] published by industry analyst firm Gartner, Inc., the authors predicted a new economy of connections. The business value of this economy of connections comes from the build out of *digital business ecosystems.*

EXHIBIT 11-1. **Supply Chain Volume Statistics**

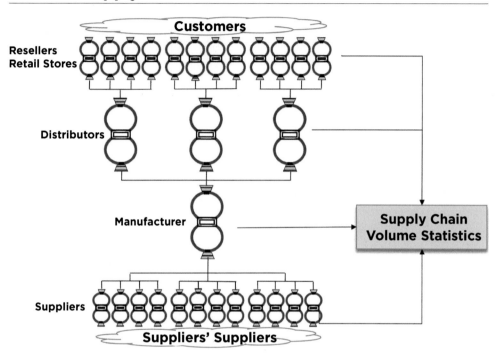

In line with this thinking, *Supply Chain Volume Statistics* is presented as a MPI—a collection of data at various points along the supply chain that is presented in a shared dashboard for all partners to see. The collective view presents the current flow volume and forecasts of upstream raw materials, production status, inventory positions, and downstream flow volume and forecasts of finished goods and services through distribution. By sharing this multiple point dashboard, all supply chain participants can easily see the status of flow/forecasts and then collaborate to solve problems and manage ecosystem operational efficiency. As stated in the Gartner article, "The data created from the ecosystem not only provides powerful knowledge about how the system acts, but also provides leading indicators to improve predictive and prescriptive analytics."

11.3 Macro Performance Indicators for Product Leadership

A product leadership value discipline can achieve a competitive advantage by *continuously developing new products and services to lead the market in innovation.* Apple has been successful in this strategy for many years, especially while under the direction of Steve Jobs. MPIs for product leadership are focused on the stream of innovations that drive revenue.

Product Leadership MPI 1—New Product Vitality Index

New Product Vitality Index (NPVI), a favorite MPI of 3M for many years, is the percentage of revenue the company generates from products that didn't exist five years earlier. As a measure of innovation output, it qualifies as an MPI that a company can use to drive investment and new techniques of innovation, excluding updates or incremental versions of existing products. As described by Inge G. Thulin, president and CEO of 3M, in 2008, 25 percent of the company's revenue came from products created in the past five years. Today, that number is 34 percent. "That's an incredible figure," Thulin said. "We are thirty billion dollars in terms of revenue as a company, meaning over ten billion dollars of the products we are selling today did not exist five years ago."[4]

Accelerating innovation in product leadership companies is a multi-functional endeavor that connects the production cycle (Research and Development) of product leadership companies (see Exhibit 10-2) to the accurate determination of customer CPV and requirements in the marketing and sales function. If done correctly, the results can be significant because new products go to market sooner, which means more lifetime revenue for the company.

Product Leadership MPI 2—Marketing and Sales Efficiency (MSE)

The MSE MPI can be applied to several value disciplines due to the importance of the sales engine in many companies, especially those with mass marketing or direct sales teams. The MSA MPI can be calculated rather simply for any size organization. Here is the formula, based on the classic efficiency formula of output divided by input:

$$MSE = \frac{Gross\ Profit}{Total\ Cost\ of\ M\&S}$$

Gross Profit is the company's gross profit for a given period

Total Cost of M&S is the cost of sales and marketing salaries, benefits, travel, entertainment, and all marketing expenses. Sales and marketing managers and vice presidents are included.

This MPI is a powerful metric that provides a clear view of the efficiency of the marketing and sales function of the value chain. Gross profit is used instead of revenue because it is a clearer factor for value sold. Tracking this MPI over time shows a trend line that indicates results when better selling techniques are leveraged, sales teams mature over time, the marketing team rolls out a winning campaign that results in increased business, or when goods and services are sold with reduced cost of goods sold or a price premium. This metric has the property of aligning multiple departments to achieve impactful results over time, and should be viewed as a lagging indicator of applied tactics.

Product Leadership MPI#3—Average Development Time (ADT)

Management of research and development is a supreme challenge considering that developers are "logical artists." The combination of logical engineering and creativity leads to lengthy development efforts and a reluctance to release their product without perfection. In addition, developers are enthusiastic when estimating development time (man months). Managers will frequently use their own factor to reach a realistic time estimate that is two to three times the original developer estimate. The development process is chaotic and uncertain with spontaneous changes as the product is created. ADT is a valuable MPI that, when plotted over time, can show improvements in the production cycle of the value chain. Improvements in ADT come from multiple functional areas of the value chain including:

- Precise product specifications from product marketing
- Reduced scope creep during the development cycle
- Faster development and testing techniques (Rapid Application Development, Agile Project Management, Extreme Project Management)

- Recruiting of top-notch talent
- Indefinite factors such as culture and inspirational leadership

Finally, ADT should be tracked separately for new product versus upgrade development, which have different constraints and challenges.

11.4 **Macro Performance Indicators for Customer Intimacy**

As seen in Exhibit 8-5, the customer intimacy value discipline strives to *continually customize products and services to meet customer-specific needs to attain customer loyalty*. In addition to the attention given to one-off custom goods and services, the lifetime value of a customer is critical to the success of this competitive strategy. Customer loyalty over time becomes the leading factor for company profitability. It is critical for the company to evaluate their customers and select those top clients for investment of time and resources to gain that loyalty. *Note*: the MPIs below are open to interpretation for application to each given company and are the likely candidates for business research.

Customer Intimacy MPI #1—Customer Investment Factor (CIF)

The customer intimacy discipline requires the company to invest in select customers to become more knowledgeable than other competitors about the customer's environment, requirements, and internal processes. Naturally, it is important to select the best customers to invest resources and time to gain that knowledge and in return receive loyalty, on-going business, and profitability. In addition, the company must have the discipline to reduce or eliminate investment in less attractive customers. Making this determination is not as hard as it seems, but it can be challenging to convince the sales organization to focus on the top customers and reduce effort on others.

A Customer Investment Factor (CIF) matrix for evaluating every customer on an annual or semi-annual basis is provided in Exhibit 11-2.

EXHIBIT 11-2. **Customer Investment Factor Matrix**

Customer Name	Business Potential ($000 over 2 yrs)	Client Relationship (Describe)	Pay on Time (Avg, Days over Payment Terms)	BP Score	CR Score	PoT Score	Grade
Customer 1	$5–8 M	Client appreciates us; is easy to work with; our sales people have access to a broad network of mgrs.	+5 days	4	5	5	A (14)
Customer 2	$1–2M	Client does not appreciate us; tough to work with; our sales people have little access to network with mgrs.	+ 40 days	2	1	1	D (4)
Customer 3	$2–5M	Client does not appreciate us; tough to work with; our sales people have some access to network with mgrs.	+ 15 days	4	1	3	C (8)
Customer 4	$500K–1M	New customer; good to work with so far; one department penetration so far	+ 10 days	2	3	4	B (9)

CIF Evaluation Exercise:

The goal of this exercise is to evaluate <u>all</u> customers at least annually to determine an overall grade of A, B, C, or D. New customers usually rate a C until more is known about them.

- **Business Potential**—The sales forecast for the next two years is entered with a range. Optional BP Score is 1-5, with 5 being the highest. Score is assigned for BP dollars relative to all other customers.

- **Client Relationship**—A description of the working relationship with 1) client perspective of the value that the company delivers; 2) ease of working together; and 3) the company's current breadth of network and ease of gaining introductions. Optional CR Score is 1-5, with 5 being the highest. CR Score of 5 is the best possible relationship/network with great ability to expand into other departments; 3 is average/neutral relationship; and 1 is negative relationship.

- **Pay on Time**—What is the client's average days over payment term for the last year. Optional PoT Score is 1-5, with 5 being the highest. A PoT Score of 5 is average 0-5 days over payment terms; 3 is 12-20 days over terms, and 1 is 30+ days over terms (adjust as needed for your company).

After the annual CIF matrix has been completed, an investment strategy can be adopted for each customer depending on their grade:

- **"A" Customers**—Invest 50-60 percent of resources and sales effort into A customers. Use strategic account management techniques to expand into new departments and opportunities. Hold regular customer discovery sessions to understand changes in their environment, their perspective, and their detailed requirements for goods and services. Educate internal departments on the needs of these clients. These are your loyal customers and they drive your profitability over time.

- **"B" Customers**—Invest 25-30 percent of resources and sales effort in B customers. The strategy is to elevate a B customer to an A over time.

- **"C" Customers**—Invest 5-10 percent of resources and sales effort in C customers. The strategy is to move these customers up or out in a specific timeframe. A collaborative session with executives on both sides can explore what it takes to strengthen the relationship and produce value for the client.

- **"D" Customers**—Do not invest in these customers. They are a drain on your resources for little to no return, which represents a bad business situation. The strategy would be to tactfully disengage from them.

The strategic level CIF evaluation provides insights that can be used to drive tactical plans across multiple departments to manage the investments over the upcoming year. To help follow improvements, the five-year revenue of each customer should be tracked on a trend line sorted by CIF grade (A, B, C, D). This gives a view of customer loyalty.

Customer Intimacy MPI #2—Marketing and Sales Efficiency (MSE)

As described in the MPIs for Product Leadership, Marketing and Sales Efficiency is a major metric that also applies to Customer Intimacy. Based on the case study of the technology reseller TRC in Chapter 10, you can see in Exhibit 11-3 an example of the trend line for MSE as this company transitioned from operation excellence to a customer intimacy value discipline at the beginning of 2010. Note that a factor of 1 means that the cost of marketing and sales just equals the gross profit sold, while a factor of 2 means that the gross profit is double the cost of marketing and sales. In the case of TRC, its shift to a customer intimacy strategy resulted in an increase in marketing and sales efficiency from 1.75 to 2.6, which brought a greater volume of gross profit into the company for the associated marketing and sales expense.

EXHIBIT 11-3. **Marketing and Sales Efficiency (MSE) for TRG Company**

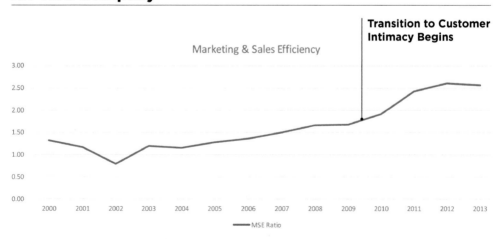

Customer Intimacy MPI #3—Net Promoter Score (NPS)

Customer satisfaction related to goods and services is especially important when following a customer intimacy value discipline. Ultimately, loyalty is derived from consistent customer satisfaction and grows from achieving the "O-Wow" factor of outstanding products and services. NPS is based on asking the customer one question with a scale of 1 to 10: "How likely is it that you would recommend our company/product/service to a friend or colleague?" Over time, an average NPS of 9-10 means that your firm should be maintaining client loyalty and gaining references for additional business. On an individual response basis, a 9-10 represents a *promoter* who is enthusiastic; a 7-8 represents a *passive customer* who is neutrally unenthusiastic and could switch to a competitor; and anything less than a 7 is considered a *detractor* who could spread negative sentiments about the company's goods and services. It is typically a good idea to provide an area for descriptive feedback along with the single question to gain context to the rating.

Customer Intimacy MPI #4—Expectation Matching Score (EMS)

A key to customer intimacy is understanding the needs and requirements of the client and then delivering goods and services that meet those specific needs. This is typical of make-to-order and engineer-to-order business models where the final outcome is typically a one-off or limited run product. To please or super-please the customer, the customer intimacy company must match or exceed the expectations of the client and hopefully doing this in an acceptable timeframe.

The Expectation Matching Score (EMS) is a simple ratio of the result versus expectation divided by the actual time versus the estimated time it took to deliver the product or service.

$$\text{EMS} = \frac{\text{Results vs Expectation}}{\text{Delivery Time Actual vs Expected}}$$

Results vs Expectation is expressed as a number with 1.0 being a perfect match of results and expectations. A number below 1 represents results lower than expected and a number higher than 1 represents results that were higher than expected. This factor may be determined by surveying the customer.

Delivery Time Actual vs Expected is expressed as a number with 1.0 being on time delivery. A number below 1 represents the delivery that was faster than estimated and a number greater than one was longer than expected.

For example, a job shop (Make to Order) works with a customer to develop a custom metal part. A specification with drawings and a 3-D model are created during the design phase. The customer approves the design, which sets the expected outcome. The job shop foreman reviews the design documents and estimates that the part can be made in two days (16 hours). As the part is being manufactured, a quality issue occurs due to a challenging Numerical Control cutting process, resulting in rework of the part. The final parts that match the specifications exactly are provided to the customer, but it took an additional two hours to complete. The EMS factor would be 1 (exact match) divided by 1.125 (18 hours divided by 16 hours), which equals 0.80 for this instance.

Although this may seem trivial to some, the power in this ratio comes from the ability to match or exceed expectations (sometimes a subjective measure) while delivering on time or faster. A focus on this metric leads a customer intimacy firm to seek out extra elements for the goods or services that please the customer beyond expectations. For example, a Mexican restaurant provides a free cup of sherbet after the meal at no charge, so the customer leaves feeling like he received something extra for his money. The delivery time on the other hand is another critical element to customer expectation and satisfaction. In this very busy world, if the company can provide a shorter *time to solution*, the customer is going to be very pleased. Finally, a company that excels at customer intimacy will have key personnel who have in-depth knowledge of the customer's current and future needs, and they can communicate the requirements for a new product or service directly to the manufacturing/delivery team so that the final outcome will match or exceed the client's expectation in a shorter time. The value of these internal customer-knowledge individuals is tremendous relative to the short-term results on the EMS scores and the long-term loyalty and profitability of strategic accounts.

11.5 Macro Performance Indicators by Value Chain Functional Elements

In Exhibit 11-4 below, the MPIs are presented and defined with a focus on the value creation capability of each major element of the value chain.

EXHIBIT 11-4. **Macro Performance Indicators for the Dynamic Value Chain**

Macro Performance Indicator	Formula	Description	Includes
Sales and Marketing	GP/Cost of Sales and Marketing	A measure of sales funnel efficiency with output (booked GP) divided by input (the cost of marketing and sales)	• Sales and Mktg personnel • All direct S&M managers • Sales travel and expenses • Marketing campaigns • PR and advertising
Order Fulfillment	Order Cycle Time	Order to Cash— The time from order received to cash received	• Order entry • Pick from inventory • Prep for shipping • Shipping to Customer Receipt • Billing • Accounts Receivable time • Cash received
Inventory	Inventory turns (COGS/Average Inventory)	Number of times per year that the inventory is sold Note: some business models do not have a physical inventory.	• COGS of products shipped • Average Inventory (beginning inventory cost + ending inventory cost divided by 2) • One year period
Production	Production Cycle Time	Work Order to Placement in Inventory —the average time of production to finished good or service	• Analysis • Design • Build • Validate—testing and QC
Procurement and Supply	Cost of Supplies & Resources/ Cost of Procurement, Transportation and Quality Rejects	A measure of the procurement funnel efficiency with output (cost of supplies and resources) divided by the input (the cost of procurement, transportation, and quality rejects)	• Production raw materials • New resources acquired for services • Procurement personnel • Procurement travel & expenses • Transportation Costs • Cost of the materials rejected for quality reasons

The MPIs presented here can be utilized in line with the specific competitive strategies of this chapter. Rather than following many department-specific KPIs, cross departmental MPIs drive impactful business optimization that leads to sustainable profitability. Additional research is encouraged to expand upon the MPI concept.

CHAPTER 12

Conclusion

THIS BOOK PRESENTS SEVERAL NEW CONCEPTS that should be useful to entrepreneurs, business practitioners, as well as academics and students. As is typical with all new business ideas, there will be debate and discussions about the concepts presented here. This is encouraged. I have found the Dynamic Value Chain to be very useful in starting new businesses and optimizing existing ones, and I want to share the knowledge that I have gained through my career that helped me understand diverse business models.

There are many interesting avenues for additional research and development associated with the Dynamic Value Chain, especially in competitive strategy and Macro Performance Indicators. I have been most excited about these MPIs because they overcome an issue with the hundreds of KPIs that are defined across every department in larger companies. The resulting siloed organization and narrow performance focus seems to be counter-productive in many companies. Using a few MPIs to direct the company performance has the potential to align and increase the impact of a competitive strategy. This approach has played out at Walmart, McDonalds, Ford and other success stories that are well documented in business literature.

Many start-up businesses are enthralled with the product idea and miss the big picture of the five major elements, including order fulfillment and production cycles, needed to create a successful business. Now they will have an advantage with a standard architecture to define their new company with a clear understanding of what it takes to build out their venture.

Finally, as a teacher of business entrepreneurship and planning, I am excited to pass along new business concepts that makes it easier for students to grasp the complexity of business structure and operational flows. Financial reports are the scoreboard of every business, but students struggle to understand how accounting ties to the real world of business activities. With the Dynamic Value Chain, students can see the clockwork of the business and how everything works together in a single big picture model. This should help them grasp the functionality of a business and what needs to be done to be successful.

References

Chapter 2

[1]Collins, J.C. and J.I. Porras, *Built to Last* (New York: HarperCollins, 1994), 22–23.

[2]Porter, M. E., *Competitive Advantage* (New York: The Free Press, 1985), 36–53.

[3]Galliers R.D. and W.R. Baets, eds., "Reflections On BPR, Information Technology and Organizational Change," in *Information Technology and Organizational Transformation: Innovation For The 21st Century Organization* (Chichester: John Wiley & Sons, 1998), 225–243.

Chapter 4

[1]Lewis, E. St. Elmo, *Financial Advertising for Commercial and Savings Banks, Trust, Title Insurance, and Safe Deposit Companies, Investment House,* (Indianapolis: Levey Bros. & Company, 1908).

Chapter 7

[1]Ament, Phil, "Assembly Line History—Invention of the Assembly Line." http://Ideafinder.com

[2]Domm, Robert W., Michigan Yesterday & Today (McGregor, MN: Voyageur Press, 2009).

[3]Kachadourian, Gail, "Ford forges dealership network." *Automotive News,* June 16, 2003. http://www.autonews.com/article/20030616/SUB/306160860/ford-forges-dealer-ship-network.

[4]Spekman, R.E. and P.W. Farris, "Designing Channels of Distribution" (Darden Business Publishing, University of Virginia, April 21, 2009), 2.

[5]Piggly Wiggly website, "About Us" section, http://www.pigglywiggly.com/about-us

[6]Peapod website, "Company Overview," http://www.peapod.com/site/companyPages/our-company-overview.jsp

[7]Ford Company website, "Rouge Factory Tour," http://www.thehenryford.org/rouge/index.aspx

[8]Drake, Matt, *Global Supply Chain Management* (Business Expert Press, 2012), 2–7.

9Cox, J.F., J.H. Blackstone, and M.S. Spencer, eds., *APICS Dictionary* (8th Edition), American Production and Inventory Control Society (Falls Church, VA, 1995).

10Forrester, J.W., *Industrial Dynamics* (Waltham, MA: Pegasus Communications, 1961).

11Forrester, J.W., "System Dynamics and the Lessons of 35 Years," in *A Systems-Based Approach to Policy Making* (Kluwer Academic Publishers 1993)

Chapter 8

1Slywotzky, Adrian J. and David J. Morrison, with Bob Adelman, *The Profit Zone: How Strategic Business Design Will Lead You to Tomorrow's Profits* (Times Business Random House: New York, 1997), 20–21.

2Elgin, Ben, "Google Buys Android for Its Mobile Arsenal." Bloomberg Businessweek. Archived from the original on February 24, 2011, http://www.webcitation.org/5wk7sIvVb.

3Wilson, Mark, "T-Mobile G1: Full Details of the HTC Dream Android Phone." Gizmodo.com, September 23, 2008. http://gizmodo.com/5053264/t-mobile-g1-full-details-of-the-htc-dream-android-phone

4Chang, Rita, "Verizon Spending $100 Million On Its Droid Ad Campaign." Businessinsider.com, November 9, 2009, http://www.businessinsider.com/verizon-spending-100-million-on-its-droid-ad-campaign-2009-11.

5Ricker, Thomas, "Jobs: App Store launching with 500 iPhone applications, 25% free." Engadget.com, July 10, 2008, http://www.engadget.com/2008/07/10/jobs-app-store-launching-with-500-iphone-applications-25-free/.

6Perez, Sarah, "iTunes App Store Now Has 1.2 Million Apps, Has Seen 75 Billion Downloads To Date." TechCrunch.com, June 2, 2014, http://techcrunch.com/2014/06/02/itunes-app-store-now-has-1-2-million-apps-has-seen-75-billion-downloads-to-date/.

7AppBrain Stats, "Number of Android Apps," September 12, 2014, http://www.appbrain.com/stats/number-of-android-apps.

8Bureau of Labor Statistics "Consumer Expenditures 2013 (USDL-14-1671)," September 9, 2014, http://www.bls.gov/news.release/cesan.nr0.htm.

9ConsumerReports.org, "What that Car Really Costs to Own," last updated August 2012, http://consumerreports.org/cro/2012/12/what-that-car-really-costs-to-own/index.htm.

10Spector, Mike, Jeff Bennett, and John D. Stoll, "U.S. Car Sales Set Records in 2105," *Wall Street Journal,* updated January 5, 2016, http://www.wsj.com/articles/u-s-car-sales-poised-for-their-best-month-ever-1451999939.

11Halberstam, David, *The Reckoning* (New York: Open Road Integrated Media, 1986) Chapter 31.

12Porter, M. E., *Competitive Strategy: Techniques for Analyzing Industries and Competitors* (New York: The Free Press, 1980).

[13]Treacy, M. and F. Wiersema, "Customer Intimacy and Other Value Disciplines." *Harvard Business Review* (January-February 1992), 84–93.

Chapter 9

[1]Collins, J. C., *Good to Great: Why some companies make the leap ... and others don't* (New York: Harper Business, 2001).

Chapter 10

[1]3M Corporation 2015 Annual Report, February 16, 2016, http://s2.q4cdn.com/974527301/files/doc_financials/2015/ar/2015_3M_Annual_Report.pdf

[2]A Century of Innovation, The 3M Story 2002 The 3M Company, http://multimedia.3m.com/mws/media/171240O/3m-coi-book-tif.pdf

Chapter 11

[1]Womack, James P., and Daniel T. Jones, *Lean Thinking* (New York: The Free Press, 2003), 352.

[2]Pieńkowski, Maciei, "Waste Management Techniques for Lean Companies," *International Journal of Lean Thinking*, December 2014, Volume 5, Issue 1.

[3]Burkett, Michael, and John Johnson, "Supply Chain 2025: Planning Today for Tomorrow," Gartner (6 July 2016)

[4]"3M CEO: Research Is 'Driving This Company,'" CNBC, June 10, 2013, http://www.cnbc.com/id/100801531.

David N. Culbreth is a highly-experienced business practioner, author and teacher living in Denver, CO. Early in his career he worked with Fortune 500 companies in the automobile, aerospace, rubber, discrete manufacturing, and oil and gas industries to design their factories and plants using computer-aided design and 3D visualization. Mr. Culbreth has held management positions in national and international software and consulting services firms, including executive director, vice president, general manager and chief operations officer. In addition to successfully creating and running business units within large corporations, he has started up entrepreneurial businesses and organizations outside of the corporation. He was a board member of a national non-profit for seven years and was elected chairman of the board.

Since 2012, Mr. Culbreth has taught entrepreneurship, business planning and operations at Colorado University Boulder, Leeds School of Business. Today, in addition to his teaching, he has founded a private research institute to provide education and promote research related to the Dynamic Value Chain and Macro Performance Indicators. (**www.DynamicValueChains.com**)

Made in the USA
Middletown, DE
29 August 2018